Tales From Africa

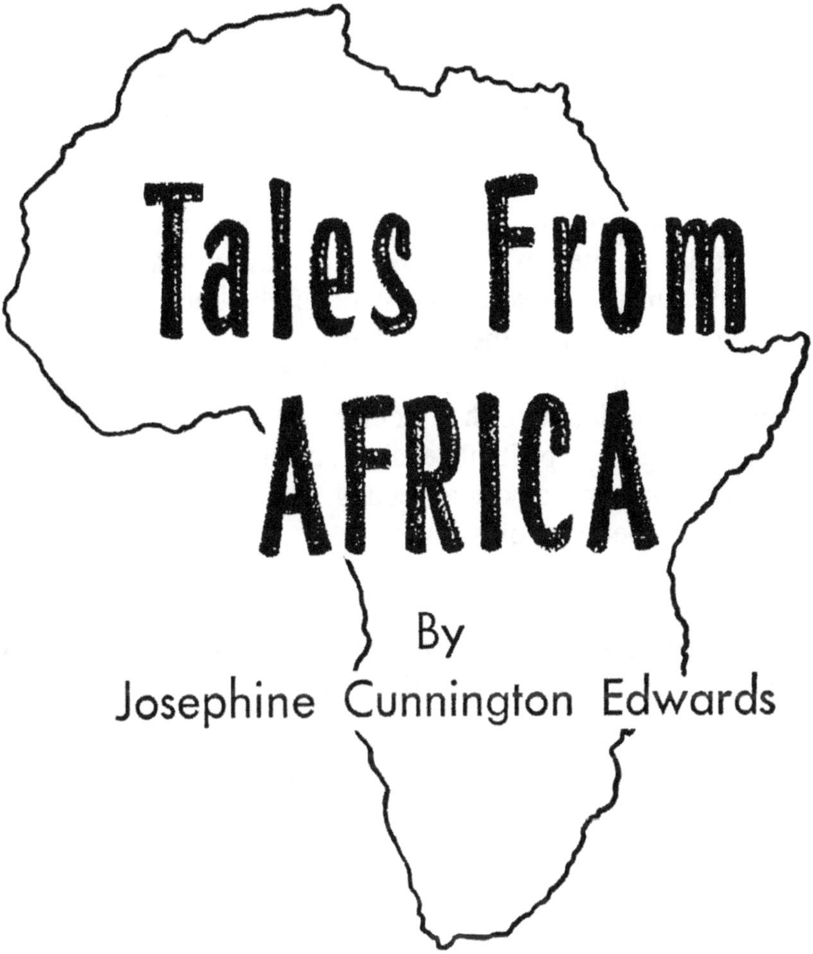

Tales From AFRICA

By
Josephine Cunnington Edwards

Illustrated by
Joseph Malmede

TEACH Services, Inc.
P U B L I S H I N G
www.TEACHServices.com • (800) 367-1844

Copyright © 2023 TEACH Services, Inc.
ISBN-13: 978-1-4796-1682-4 (Paperback)

Published by

TEACH Services, Inc.
P U B L I S H I N G
www.TEACHServices.com • (800) 367-1844

Foreword

Come, children, come, every one of you, and gather around my feet. The fire is blazing up in my fireplace, and it is damp and cold here at Malamulo Mission in Nyasaland. I have many stories to tell you about how boys and girls live in Africa. Their lives are different from yours; you can be sure of that. But they are interesting just the same.

Are you surprised that I have a fire in my house in Africa? You thought it was hot all the time, didn't you? Well, it *is* hot sometimes. In September, October, and November it is extremely hot. The winds blow, but they almost wither a person up, they are so hot.

Then, there is no rain, and everything is dry. Even the lawns are an ugly dry brown. The streams dry up, until the poor creatures of the woods have to hunt and hunt for a drink of water. Our own drinking water in the big cisterns is low and dirty. Then—we can't help it—we begin to think of the cool water from the deep wells in the homeland.

The wondrous heavy rains begin to fall in November. The people are happy. They all, even the boys and girls, go out into the gardens to help plant corn, beans, cabbages, and cucumbers. They also plant cassava, a root from which tapioca is made. When the roots are boiled, they become snowy white and taste something like potatoes.

5

After a while May comes, bringing cold, miserable rains. The native people call the steady misty rains *ciperoni*. The air is full of moisture. Even the blankets on the beds feel damp. I build a big fire in my fireplace and feel sorry for the thousands of people who are too poor to own a blanket. I begin to pray, and I pray for Jesus to come because there is so much suffering and sickness. Many of the little babies and the old, weak people get sick and die. We hear the people in the villages crying and crying.

I think then of the verses in Isaiah telling about the beautiful earth made new. He said that the "ransomed of the Lord" would live in a beautiful place, and sorrow and sighing would be no more.

So, get ready, dear children, for Auntie Jo wants you to hear stories of swift rivers, prowling lions, hissing snakes, and crocodiles. When you hear these stories, know this: Every one is a true story, and it has happened to the boys and girls who came to my classes from all over the country of Nyasaland. Are you ready? Get settled then, and don't go to sleep!

Lovingly,
Auntie Jo

Contents

He Slept in a Tree

SOSOLA received a sad letter from home one day. His dear mother, who had been sick for a long time, had just died. It is the custom in Africa to bury people on the same day that they die, so of course poor Sosola could not hope to get home in time for the funeral. There were many long miles of wild bush to go through.

His heart was so sad when he got the letter that he didn't eat one bite of food before he started for his home early the next morning. He got a ride into Blantyre, a city about forty miles from Malamulo; but there were still about ninety long miles of wild, rough country ahead before he could reach Matandani Mission, which was his home. Some way, he managed to get to Chileka Mission, which is about seventy-five miles from Matandani.

I am sure that his friends at Chileka would have given him food if they had known he hadn't eaten that day, but Sosola was so sad that he did not once think of food.

Birks Kalulu, one of the teachers at Chileka, came forward to meet the boy. "Oh, Sosola," he said kindly, "we truly sympathize with you in your sorrow. We heard the news today. How are you getting home?"

"I do not know," Sosola answered sadly. "But I do want

to get home today if possible, so I can comfort my poor father."

Birks looked at the sun.

"If you take my bicycle and ride very fast, you can get there before night," he said. "But you must hurry. Do not delay for a minute."

Within five minutes Sosola was speeding down the narrow, rough road on Teacher Birks's bicycle. Only then did he think of food. It was long past noon, and his stomach was calling loudly for food. And when a small hill loomed before him, Sosola was so weak from grief and hunger he could hardly push the bike up it.

Even though he was a big boy, he could not keep from crying.

"Oh, Mother, Mother," he sobbed as he thought of the many times he had eaten the delicious savory food prepared by her loving hands.

The farther he went, the rougher the road was, and the weaker he grew. The sun sank lower and lower until the thick bush was only in half light. A new danger threatened the boy. He knew that at the hour of twilight lions, leopards, and hyenas go forth to search for food.

As if giving voice to his fear, a lion roared, far away. The poor lad almost fainted from fear. Matandani was still nine long miles away over the roughest and wildest kind of road. It was eleven miles back to the nearest village.

Then Sosola took his bicycle and leaned it up against a tall tree. It took all his strength to climb up the thick trunk. Then he took a rope and tied himself to a little basketlike formation of limbs and prepared to spend the night. Before he went to sleep up in his high bed, he said his prayers just as his dear mother had taught him when he was small. Once he heard a lion roar near at hand, but he knew that God

Sosola took his bicycle and leaned it up against a tall tree. It took all his strength to climb up.

would take care of him, so he was not afraid. When he awoke, the sun was shining brightly all about him. He untied the rope and got ready to get down. Just then, across the path, he spied a mango tree laden heavy with rich, ripe yellow fruit. The Lord had set a table for him in the wilderness. Gladly he descended and ate his fill before he went on to Matandani to comfort his father, and to be comforted himself.

Adventures of Mtambo

TO LOOK at Mtambo sitting quietly in the middle of the classroom at Malamulo, one would find it hard to believe he had experienced so many adventures. But Mtambo has had a most thrilling life and has faced death several times. The first time was when he was just a baby, learning to walk. Every night his brother went to the cattle kraal to milk the cow. One evening he begged the mother to let him take baby Mtambo along.

"Now you be careful of this baby, you boy," the mother warned. Away went big brother Ntokoloza, leading the naked black baby by the hand.

The big brother set the small, fat little fellow on the other side of the cow. Ntokoloza set the clay pot under the old cow's udder and began milking.

But the cow did not enjoy having a boy on each side of her, and suddenly she began to thrash around, jumping this way and that. Suddenly she stumbled and fell heavily on poor baby Mtambo.

Ntokoloza began to jump up and down and to scream at the top of his voice. He was *sure* Mtambo must be dead. The father, mother, aunts, uncles, and the old grandmother —all came running.

All together they lifted the heavy cow and pulled little Mtambo out. He was limp and seemed to be hardly breathing. His heathen mother did not know what to do. She walked up and down holding the baby, who did not cry or open his eyes. There were no doctors near at all, so she did not know anything to do but call a witch doctor. He brewed a smelly, horrible mess of strange medicine and tried to give it to the baby. Then he made a terrific uproar, shaking rattles and banging around, dancing and jumping. But little Mtambo didn't hear a thing. He was sick and near death for nearly six months. But at last he got well.

The House Burns

When Mtambo was about four years old, his mother put him and his brothers and sisters to bed on their mats one night. Then she and the other heathen slipped away from the house to go to a beer dance in a nearby village.

Poor little Mtambo had not wanted to go to bed at all that night, for his mother had not cooked a bit of supper. All the children were crying with hunger.

"Cete!" shouted the heathen mother. She loved beer so much that she did not want to take time to cook. That is why she said, "Cete." That means, "You shut up." So the little black children cried in the darkness until they went to sleep, and the mother and father went to the beer dance.

Did you ever see a beer dance? It is not a pretty sight. The drums just beat and beat, and the people jump and leap and dance around the fires until the sweat runs down their bodies in streams. They stop often to drink some of the sour beer, frothy and bubbling in big pots under the eaves of the native huts.

You can hear the pounding of the bare feet on the ground and the shrill crying for a long distance. After this heathen

13

mother and father became terribly drunk and foolish, they decided to go home. They stumbled, staggered, and fell down so often that it took a long time for them to make it. By the time they got home, they were both hungry but still very drunk. Their little children lay asleep on the dirty mats.

"I will cook *nsima*," muttered the drunk mother. "I will make a big, big fire, so I can cook it quickly," she added foolishly. The father decided to visit some friends and left.

Then the mother went out and got a great high heap of dry grass and put it in a pile right in the center of the mud hut. She got the pot, the water, the meal, and the stirring stick. Then she went out to try to find a live coal. She wandered up and down near the neighbors' cookhouses, till at last she found a coal under a pile of ashes. Hurriedly putting this on some leaves, she ran home to kindle her fire.

The heathen mother was so drunk and foolish that she did not realize her children were in terrible danger.

Suddenly the fire roared up with a great blaze, scaring the drunk woman so much that she ran out of the house. She closed the door, too, leaving her little ones in there with the terrible fire.

If the neighbors had not come and rescued little Mtambo and his brothers and sisters, they would have died. The house burned up. The heathen mother was so drunk and foolish that she did not realize her children were in terrible danger. This was the second time poor Mtambo came near to death. Surely God had a work for him, or he would not have been saved.

Mtambo's Enemies

One day, about two years after the fire, Mtambo and his brother M'Mussa went to the bush to hunt birds and mice with two other village boys. All the boys carried knobkerries, or sticks with a hard knot of wood on the end. They could throw these very skillfully and kill animals and birds from quite a distance.

Mtambo and M'Mussa were luckier than their friends. M'Mussa espied a rabbit, which he killed by throwing his knobkerrie. He later killed another one the same way. Little Mtambo killed a wild guinea fowl. The other boys, who had killed only mice and birds, were jealous. And because they were bigger, they began to quarrel with the two younger boys, demanding their game. Of course M'Mussa and Mtambo refused, for they liked to eat rabbit meat and were looking forward to a good meal. Presently the older boys pretended that they had forgotten about the rabbits. They pointed to a nest in a high tree.

"You, M'Mussa," they said. "You are a small one. It is good for you to go up there and get the eggs for us to eat. They will taste good with *nsima*."

Without suspecting their naughty purposes, M'Mussa laid his rabbits down on the ground and started climbing the tree. Immediately the wicked boys gathered much dry grass and dry wood and began to build an immense fire all around the tree.

"We are going to cook you," they shouted. "We want to eat your rabbits!" So, leaving M'Mussa up in the tree over the big hot fire, they grabbed his rabbits and ran. But little Mtambo began to cry. The bad boys then took Mtambo's guinea fowl and led him to a place where an animal had burrowed a hole deep in the hillside.

"You get in there," they shouted. "If we let you go home, you will tell what we did to your brother." So they pushed poor little Mtambo deep into the hole. Then they built another fire in front of that hole, so he could not get out.

Poor little Mtambo! He would have surely died there of the smoke and heat if the hole had not been burrowed far into the hillside. The little black child crept as far into the hole as he could, but he soon fainted from the effects of the smoke and the heat.

Meanwhile those bad boys arrived in the village with their birds, mice, guinea fowl, and the two rabbits. They took these directly to their mother's hut.

"See, Amai? Much *nyama!*" they said.

Their mother was glad to see that these boys had brought home so much meat, and began to praise them loudly.

Just then there came Mtambo and M'Mussa's father and mother.

"Where are our sons?" they cried. "Where are they? We know they went hunting with you two boys!"

The boys looked down at the ground.

"They did not go with us," they muttered. You could see the boys were afraid.

"Yes, they did; we saw them going with you. Now, where are they?"

"They left us and went another way," they said; but the way they said it, it was plain they were telling lies.

Then the father and the mother and many of the villagers went in search of the missing boys. They were all suspicious, for those other boys were known to be full of evil tricks.

"I see smoke," cried Mtambo's mother. "Let us run. I feel it in my bones that my children are in danger!"

They quickened their footsteps until they came first to the fire the boys had made by Mtambo. The child was moaning, and the quick ear of the mother heard him. The fire was drawn away quickly, and the father crept into the burrow and drew his little child out. He was unconscious and lay as if he were dead. Then they carried him to the side of a little stream and washed his face. When he was able to speak and understand, he led them to the tree. Little M'Mussa had given up hope and was weeping bitterly. The logs the boys had dragged up to the tree to burn were still blazing brightly. Soon M'Mussa was saved, and an angry group swept into the village. The bad boys saw them coming, so they ran off to the bush to hide.

The parents reported the matter to the big chiefs; and there was a big *mlandu,* or native court case, over the thing.

The parents of the bad boys had to give Mtambo's father and mother two big fat cows because of the mischief of their naughty boys. There was anger and quarreling between those families for many years.

One Is Taken, the Other Left

It is the custom in some of the African tribes for the boys to have a "sleeping house" and for the girls to have a "sleeping house," away from the house of the parents.

2

One night two little boys came to visit Mtambo and M'Mussa. They played many games in the darkness of the *bwalo,* or courtyard; then they ate and went to bed. Mtambo remembers that there was a good supper that night. The mother had cooked rice; and there was a delicious relish made of onions, tomatoes, and cabbage. They all ate until they were full and happy.

Since the night was warm, the boys pulled their mats up close to the door. Mtambo and the smaller boy were on one mat, and M'Mussa and his friend were on the other. Later in the night Mtambo felt a fierce tugging at the blanket. It was getting colder and he held on, crying out, "Don't pull off the covers! Don't pull off the covers!"

But suddenly the other little boy let out a terrible cry, and Mtambo sat up sleepily. Where, oh, where was that blanket? Then he became wide awake, for a great leopard was dragging his little friend across the *bwalo* where they had played so happily only that evening.

"Amai! Bambo!" he screamed. "Amai! Bambo!" Out ran the mother and father. Torches were lit, and the whole village set out after the big cat. They shouted as they ran, hoping to scare the leopard and save the little lad's life.

They did scare the leopard. But it was too late. Mtambo's little friend was dead. Mtambo cried loudly as he stood there looking at him.

"It might have been *me!*" he sobbed. "Oh, Amai! It might have been me!"

Mtambo is now a grown man and ready to go out as a teacher. He wants to be a good teacher, for he believes that God has helped him many, many times and saved his life.

Lovewell's Two Fearful Adventures

ISN'T Lovewell a strange name? Lovewell Kaonga is a student at Malamulo Mission. He came from far north of Nyasaland, where there are many big snakes and fearful wild beasts. All little Lovewell's life he heard wild beasts cry near his home at night. He used to tremble and cry out when the ground nearly shook with the roar of a dreadful lion.

Lovewell's parents were ignorant and did not realize that they ought to send him to school. They just thought that what was good enough for them was good enough for Lovewell. So the little lad was sent out to herd cattle instead of going to school. Day after day he herded the cattle near the places of water, because the grass grew greener there. But he was always fearful; for he knew that hungry lions, leopards, or hyenas might any day attack his herd. He always carried a spear and a strong knobkerrie.

One day he was herding the cattle and going round and round the herd as he always did. Suddenly his heart quaked, for a fearful roar nearly shook the earth. From the dense bush there leaped a huge male lion, the saliva dripping from his ferocious teeth. He leaped upon a fine young bull, and both went down together.

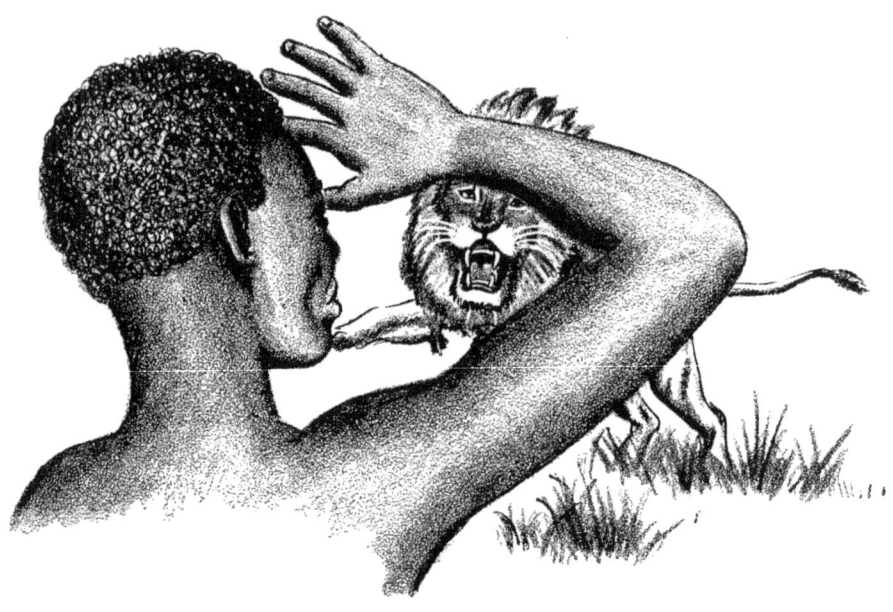

From the dense bush there leaped a huge male
lion, the saliva dripping from his ferocious teeth.

Lovewell was very much afraid, oh, yes, but he knew he
ought to take care of his father's cattle. It was his job, and
Lovewell was a trustworthy boy. Almost before he had time
to think of what he was doing, his knobkerrie whistled
through the air and struck the mighty king of the forest
right on the head. With a mighty roar of rage, the lion left
the bull and leaped at Lovewell, pinning the terrified black
boy to the ground.

In that dreadful moment Lovewell thought his hour had
come. Giant paws were on his shoulders, the lion's hot
breath nearly choked him, and the saliva dripped right into
his face.

But God in His heaven looked down upon Lovewell in
great pity. The first roar of the lion had been heard by a
hunter, who was near at hand in the bush. Fearlessly he
strode toward the place of the uproar. He parted the bushes

just as the lion leaped upon the young boy. Lightning quick he flung his razor-sharp spear at the fearful creature. The spear found the heart of the angry lion, and Lovewell was saved.

Lovewell's Kindness

One day Lovewell and his cousin started toward Lake Nyasa to go swimming. It was a fearfully hot day, and the boys were eager to enjoy the cool bath. They were trotting along happily. Just as they came in sight of Lake Nyasa, they met an old man trying to carry a heavy sack of fish. The man could hardly walk, the load was so heavy. Sweat poured from his face. He looked at the boys.

"Please, boys," he began, "won't you help me? I have been sick, and I can hardly carry my fish."

"No, we won't," shouted the cousin rudely. "We are going to go swimming. We haven't any need to help you. It is your load. Carry it yourself."

"Why, cousin, that is a bad way to talk to any old man who is sick," protested Lovewell. "Come; let's help him. We can always go swimming."

"If you want to be a fool, go on," jeered the cousin. "As for me, I'm going swimming." And away he went whistling down toward the bright waters of the lake.

Lovewell turned and took the heavy bag of fish onto his young shoulders.

"Yes, Grandfather," he answered. "I will help you. I am strong; I will carry the fish."

So Lovewell, instead of enjoying the refreshing exercise of a swim, went to the village with the weak old man and carried his load for him. The fish smelled bad in the hot sun, and dirty, foul juice dripped out of the wet sack and rolled down Lovewell's hot back. But his heart was light, for he knew that he was doing the good and right thing.

When they arrived, Lovewell was given water with which to bathe. When he had washed, good food was ready for him. The old man gave the boy three shillings for his kind deed. Just as he was getting ready to go home, he heard a great shout. A large group of boys was down the road. As they drew near, he saw that they were carrying his cousin, the one who had gone to the lake instead of helping the old man.

"Wait, Lovewell," they shouted. "You are lucky that you did not go to the pool today. We told your cousin to stay out, for a crocodile was seen there. He laughed at us and jumped in. The crocodile caught him right away. If we hadn't been there, he would have been eaten. We speared the old fellow to death and saved your cousin."

Lovewell stood looking at his cousin lying there slashed, bruised, and bleeding.

"Cousin," he said, "you should have come with me."

"Yes, I know," answered the cousin weakly. "You did right, Lovewell. I did wrong and was punished. I'll be kind after this."

Crocodile's Tail

IN THE training class at Malamulo, sitting on the back seat, is a young boy named Lassell Kaunda. He has a friendly black face and can smile happily.

Before he came the long five hundred miles down to Malamulo from Northern Nyasaland, a fearful thing happened to him. He went one day to visit his uncle, whose hut was close to beautiful Lake Nyasa. The boy thought it would be wonderful if he could live near the lake so he could go swimming every day.

When evening came on, his aunt began to get supper ready. Do you know what supper is in this queer country? It is usually a thick corn-meal mush, called *nsima,* and something else, called *ndiwo.* They roll the *nsima* into little balls the size of pigeon eggs and then dip them into the *ndiwo* before they pop the balls into the mouth. Sometimes the *ndiwo* is cabbage, or beans, or tomatoes; then again it may be mice, rats, and beetles. Meat and fish are often used for supper too.

Not far from the uncle's house was a little cove where the fishermen came in, and every evening it was possible to get fish, provided one had a little money.

But let us get back to Lassell. Soon the aunt called, "This

nsima is almost ready now. I hear the fishermen coming, so it is the time to go and get some fish for *ndiwo*."

With that, Lassell and his uncle started down to the shore to get fish. The fishermen had such a big load of fine fish that they were having trouble with the boat.

So Lassell and his uncle jumped into the water to help them. Just then Lassell felt a big body glide past him under the water, and suddenly he was hit so hard that he fainted. He did not know that crocodiles often hit people hard with their great ugly tails, then grab them with their horrible teeth.

Lassell's uncle and some of the other men seized him and ran to the shore with him. Some of the men fought the angry crocodile with sharp spears. The uncle carried Lassell to the house and laid him on a mat. He was unconscious for about ten minutes.

When he woke up, the fish was cooking, and it smelled good. Even though his back hurt very much, he sat up and ate a big supper.

Saved for a Reason

FILEMON Mwaterah is a slender, happy African boy who works in the gardens at Malamulo. He knows how to hoe with the big, clumsy, ugly hoes that are made in this country. But it is a great wonder that he is attending school at Malamulo Mission, for he had a narrow escape from death when he was a young boy.

Filemon had a fine dog, named Chobo, of which he was proud. Very often Filemon brought food home for his family because his dog was such a fine hunter. He caught guinea fowls, little bucks, and rabbits. He often caught the ugly *nyenga,* which often seized his mother's hens and slit their throats.

One day Filemon took Chobo, his spear, and his bow and arrows and went to the bush to hunt. The dog ran here and there, barking with funny little yips and yowls. Filemon ran after him as fast as his small black legs could carry him. Suddenly a deer, slender and beautiful, sprang out of the dense bush and bounded away.

"Yip! Yip! Yip! Yip!" Chobo sprang after the lovely creature, and away they went like the wind, crashing through bushes and the tall grass as if nothing were there. Filemon followed as well as he could.

After ten or fifteen minutes of swift pursuit, the deer was caught and killed. Filemon was happy. He was glad he was a strong boy; otherwise he could not have carried the deer on his shoulders. Already he was thinking of how his mother and father would praise him, and how all the villagers would boast that they had such a good boy hunter.

The load was heavy, and the sun was so hot that the sweat poured from the boy in a stream. He could hardly stagger along, the deer was so heavy. Just when he was walking through the grasses almost within sight of his

He first heard a rustling; then a long, loath-some body shot up like lightning right at him.

village, he heard a rustling at first; then a long, loathsome body shot up like lightning right at him. The next moment he felt horrible scaly folds thrown around his body in a loose, hideous coil.

A python! Only bush people know the dreadful strength of these mighty constricting serpents. Filemon never knew quite how he escaped, but he leaped clear with a terrible cry that brought the villagers running. And the great serpent glided away and escaped. God had saved His small black boy.

Now Filemon is a young man, and he is soon to go out to be a teacher. We often wonder why it is that God saves us so many times. But we are sure that God saved Filemon so that he could go out and do a mighty work for Him.

Jefty Blanket

JEFTY BLANKET has such a pleasant face that when you see him smiling all the time, you begin to smile too. He is ragged, poor, and needy, but, oh, so energetic, so dependable, and so happy. He goes to school in the morning and works for the school in the afternoon; after that he goes up to one of the mission houses to earn a little extra money for needed clothing. He is not lazy—oh, no. He is full of ambition, and he longs to be a teacher someday.

Last summer after Jefty had gotten through with his school at Matandani Mission, he went home to his own village for the vacation. His mother, in her humble way, tried to fix her sweet boy just the food he liked best. But he couldn't rest or lie around and be lazy as many other boys like to do. The first morning he arose early and went straight to his mother, who was returning from the waterside with a pot of water.

"Amai," he said, "I must make money. I need more clothing and a blanket to take to Malamulo this fall. I must work."

"Maic!" cried the mother. "Can't you rest a day or a week even? The rats are chewing your heels all the time.

Oh, well, go. I will fix you some *cimanga* and some *nsima* to carry with you. Where are you going, and what are you going to do, Jefty?"

"Amai, I'm going to Lake Nyasa to buy fish; then I'm going to take the fish and sell them at a profit. I will keep that business up all vacation."

"Maie!" cried the mother. "Was ever such a cricket born to any other woman? Go then. Jump and jump and jump. I can't keep you still. But be careful, you; there are leopards, hyenas, and hungry lions everywhere. You'll get eaten up, you will see. Then what good will all your work do?"

His blanket was tied in a flat roll which fastened to his lunch parcel. He quickly put them onto his woolly head, and away he went at a brisk trot through the rough bush to Lake Nyasa. The journey was long and the road was hot and stony. There were two streams and the Shire River to cross. He was glad that a bridge now lay across the swift-flowing waters, for he knew that crocodiles were there, waiting to champ ugly teeth onto some victim. Fifty years ago his grandfather would never have attempted to cross the river. It would have meant certain death.

After several days of walking, the lad came into sight of the lovely purling waters of the lake. Rough dugouts were bobbing like fragile eggshells on the bright waters of the bay. Other fishermen were sorting fish; some were fixing big rents in their homemade nets.

Since it was not long till nightfall, the lad decided to wait until early morning to get his fish, probably from fishermen who caught them during the night. Then they would not spoil before he could sell them. He looked about a little for a "rest house," a hut built to shelter traveling African people. He needed a place to lay his blanket down, and there he could sleep. He found a filthy hut, but since he knew ticks abounded there, he stayed out in the open. He had once felt the agonies of tick typhus, and he did not want to go through such an experience again.

Under a big baobab tree he swept a place clean with a broom made of twigs. Then gathering grass, he bunched it up until he had a soft bed of which he was proud. He ate some of the food his mother prepared, bought and cooked a fat fish, and then sluiced his hot, sweaty body with cool lake water. How good he felt!

Then, because darkness had fallen, he took off his travel-stained shirt and trousers and washed them. He knew they would be dry by morning. He was asleep almost as soon as he lay down, but a few minutes later he wakened suddenly. Somebody was shaking him.

"Boy! Boy! What are you doing here?"

"I'm sleeping," he replied stupidly. "I came to buy fish."

"Well, you are just lucky I had to come down for water. If a crocodile will not find you, a lion will."

Wrapping himself in his blanket, he took up his belongings and followed the village woman. She let him sleep on a mat spread out in her kitchen house. It was not long till he was asleep again. But about midnight he awoke again, all atremble. The ground seemed to quiver with the roaring of a lion. Shaking with fear, he arose and opened the frail little bamboo door and peered out.

The moon was shining brightly, throwing into relief every object on the beach. The baobab tree stood there, a gigantic silhouette against the white sand of the shore. Under the tree, pawing the grass of his improvised bed, were four big lions. Their manes were bristling, and they kept up a regular chorus of blood curdling roars.

Then the boy began to tremble violently. Sweat poured

from his young body in a stream. He realized now truly the truth of the memory verse, *"Mngelo wa Yehova azinga kuwacinjiriza iwo akuopa Iye, nawalanditsa iwo."*

Only *we* would say, "The angel of the Lord encampeth round about them that fear him, and delivereth them."

Daniel of Mwami

DANIEL is a student at Malamulo Mission in Nyasaland, Africa. He isn't very tall, and you would guess that he is perhaps thirteen or fourteen years old. You would be astonished to know he is nearly nineteen. He is studying psychology, principles of teaching, history of education, and school methods. He wants to be a teacher someday.

Several years ago he was a student at Mwami Mission near Fort Jameson in Northern Rhodesia. It is situated in quite a wild and unsettled part of the country, and Daniel has often heard lions roar in the night. Somehow he felt he would be safe because he had given his heart to God, and he wanted to prepare to do the work of God in preparing his people for Jesus' coming.

At the missions in Africa it is often the custom to hang a bell up in a tree. From there the boys can ring it, so that everyone can hear. One day the boys were set to work cutting the grass around the church and the school. Daniel went with them. The boys use just pieces of old strap iron to cut the grass. They have to wrap one end with old rags for a handle, then bend over and whack and whack to cut the big tufts of tough grass. It makes the poor black backs

Suddenly he heard a voice, a strange, queer voice.
It spoke directly in his ear: "Jump, Daniel! Jump!"

ache very much. After a while Daniel was cutting directly under the tree where the heavy bell hung.

"Whack! Whack! Whack!" The crude knives seemed to slash in unison. The sun was hot. Daniel could feel the sweat trickling down his back. Just then he straightened up to rest his aching muscles. Suddenly he heard a voice, a strange, queer voice. It spoke directly in his ear: "Jump, Daniel! Jump!"

The boy was so startled he gave a frantic leap, but not a second too soon. White ants had eaten the crude bell rope and caused the bell to fall heavily right where he had stood —so near that the iron grazed his shirt. If he had been standing there, the bell would have cut him in two.

3

The boys all shouted when they saw him jump and saw the heavy bell fall.

"Did you hear it, Daniel? Did you see it start to fall?" they asked curiously.

"No, I didn't. I heard a voice. The voice said, 'Jump,' and I jumped."

"It must have been an angel, Daniel. God saved you."

Daniel thinks so, too.

Nicker's Two Lions

THE NAME Nickers Chintsanya sounds funny, but it is the name of a tall, black African boy in Nyasaland. He is in school at the Malamulo Mission.

Several years ago Nickers, with two other boys, started to go on the long journey from a village called Lisungwi to Chileka Mission. Of course they had to walk, for there was no other way to go. The country between these places is quite wild, and few people live there. There are just tall grass and thick forests, which are the homes of poisonous snakes, lions, elephants, and other wild animals.

Nickers was only a small boy at the time. He had never seen a lion or a leopard, but he had heard them cry and roar at night, and he had heard the old folks tell frightening stories about wild beasts when they gathered at nighttime around the big fire.

So away these boys trotted, anxious to get to Chileka, where friends and relatives lived and where they expected to have a good time. Presently they got to the midst of a big forest. The grass stood ten feet tall on each side of the pathway. They could hear monkeys jumping from tree to tree chattering angrily.

The boys were laughing gaily when suddenly the two

older boys stopped talking. For right by the side of the road sat two big lions, a male and a female. They looked just like friendly house cats, and they were so sleepy their faces even looked kind. Even though those boys went very near, the old lions did not do a thing. The boys were sure the lions could hear the beating of their scared hearts. Just as the boys passed by, the female lion rubbed her head against the bushy mane of the male. It was just as if she said, "We are full of food, so let us not harm these boys."

You see, there is a tradition, which has been handed down from generation to generation, that it is the female lion that decides whether to attack an enemy. So when these boys saw that mother lion rub her face against the male lion, they were sure that she was telling her husband to let those boys alone.

They looked back once and then hastened on. They surely loved that old mother for letting them live and go on to Chileka for their visit.

Grace Purchase

MORE than fifty years ago a sweet young woman of about twenty-five was sent as a missionary to Africa from England. Those were hard days for strong men, but they were harder yet for young Grace Page. She had to sail a long time before she got to Africa; then she had to journey several days in a slow boat up the Zambesi River till she came to the swift waters of the wicked Shire River. The young girl knew very well that the water was full of crocodiles that would not hesitate to eat her if they got a chance. At last the slow steamer stopped at Chiromo, and there Grace was met by one of the teachers of the Zambesi Mission. There were many half-naked young men there, too, and a peculiar hammock woven out of rough grasses. The natives called this hammock a *machila*. Grace got into the *machila* and was carried all the way to the Zambesi Mission, near Blantyre, Nyasaland.

She was put to work at once, teaching little native boys. One day a handsome young man came down to Blantyre from Northern Rhodesia. His name was Harvey Purchase. As soon as he saw Grace Page, he knew that he wanted to marry her. And she immediately liked him, too.

It was not long until there was a wedding, and Grace and

Harvey were married. The young husband was an engineer and was building the first government offices in faraway Fort Jameson in Northern Rhodesia.

It took them a long time to get to their new home from Blantyre. There were no roads, and there were many wild beasts, but that was not the worst danger. The fierce Angoni tribes wandered all through this part of the country, and it was very dangerous. Many people had been killed.

At last they got there, and they bargained with the government for five thousand acres of land at about twelve and a half cents an acre. They named the place Chadzombe, which means "the place of the locust." But really it should have been called Chamikango, or "the place of lions," for lions were a great worry to these young people. Mr. Purchase shot and poisoned many of them, but they were still troublesome. All the cattle, sheep, and goats had to be locked up tightly before evening, or there would have been none of them left. No human being dared to walk outside after nightfall. How would you have liked to live at Chadzombe? I am sure you would have been scared indeed.

But little children lived there, for Grace and Harvey had three little children. They were happy together; for the mother, father, and little children all loved one another very much. One day a great sorrow came to this little family. The father swallowed an orange seed and became seriously ill. By the time a doctor arrived, it was too late and the good father had died. Now Grace and the three little children were left all alone on a big wild farm.

Many people thought Grace would take her little ones and go back to England after that, but she didn't. She loved Chadzombe, for it was home to her. She did not forget that she had come out as a missionary. She walked many miles to help the sick and needy. She taught natives to sew on the sewing machine, so that the half-naked people could have clothing. She taught others to make mattresses, so that money could be earned.

She was brave too. One day an Angoni hunter was brought to the mission. A leopard had attacked him and clawed and bitten his arm terribly. Grace saw that unless she took off the arm, the man would die. So she did a brave thing. She had him laid on a table covered with a clean sheet, and this brave woman cut off the poor African man's arm and saved his life.

One evening Grace had gathered her little children all around the table, and they were eating supper. The door to the big veranda was closed, but it was not latched. Suddenly they heard the door slowly open, as if someone were

When they turned to look, there stood a big lion in the opened door. No one said a word.

pushing it. They were all surprised, for there were no neighbors, and people did not go visiting at night.

When they turned to look, there stood a big lion in the opened door. No one said a word. The lion blinked his eyes at the lantern and came into the room like a big curious cat. He walked around the table one time; then he went out into the night.

This was the strangest visitor the Purchase children ever had. They carefully closed the door every night after that. They did not want Mr. Lion to call again.

Little Watch Girl

THE TALL corn was tasseled beautifully all around the village. The ears were big, green, and fat, promising many a dish of good *nsima* later on when the harvest was over. But there were enemies all through the bush to be conquered, or hunger would stalk through all the villages like leopards and kill everyone, big and small.

These enemies were the monkeys and the baboons, who like green corn just as well as do the African people. They can spoil a fine cornfield in an hour if they are not chased away. Because of this menace it is a common sight to see odd little huts perched on high poles just like little doll houses on stilts with coolie hats on their heads. All through the ripening season someone has to stay in them to chase away the chattering thieves that come to steal the fresh corn. It is tiresome business, and the family has to take turns. Stones and sticks must be gathered to throw, and there is no time for play while the watchers are up high in the lookout.

So in old Bambo Matuselah's family, everyone took his turn watching the *chimanga,* or the corn, when it began to ripen. Even small, weak Elida had to take her little turn. When her parents called, "Elida, Elida, it is your turn to watch the *chimanga,*" she had to go, even though she was afraid of the big hairy baboons. Some of them were as large as she was, and they scared her terribly sometimes. When she threw stones or sticks at the big old grandfathers, they seemed to know she was small and weak, and they refused to move. They would break off big fat ears of corn and eat them right in front of her. Sometimes they bared their ugly yellow teeth and chattered angrily when a stone or a clod which she threw hit them.

One day while she was watching the *chimanga,* a great crowd of huge baboons trooped into the garden and started right in breaking off the biggest ears. She screamed, called for help, and threw all her sticks and stones. Then down the ladder she scrambled, her small heart almost paralyzed with fear. Into her small *nsaru* cloth she quickly gathered stones and clods and sticks.

"*Coka! Coka iwe!*" she shouted with all her strength. She threw her ammunition as she ran.

Some of the smaller baboons and monkeys ran away, but two big fellows, as large as Elida herself, snarled angrily and started toward the small girl. Poor little Elida! She knew they could catch her and kill her easily, then return to their feast of *chimanga.* She turned to run, quite beside herself with fear.

Elida was a little Christian. Her father and mother had given up heathenism long before and had taught her to pray to the living God. So between the rows of green *chimanga* she knelt down to pray. You would not understand her prayer even if it were written down for you to read, for it was in the Chinyanja language. Even though she called the dear God "Mulungu," and said *thandiza* instead of "help," and *thawitsa* for "chase," the heavenly Father understood her; and He *did* send help to chase away the ugly thieves.

When she opened her eyes, lo, they all were gone. The corn waved sweetly in the gentle breezes, and big puffy clouds sailed high up in the sky.

Little Elida climbed up again into the high baboon lookout. She was happy, for she knew that the dear Jesus was watching over her.

The Lions and the Bicycle

CHIPUNGU was an African boy who lived in a heathen village. He had no clothes at all for a long time. One day, however, he was given a small loincloth. But he did not like it very much. It was warm where he lived, and he could run and play all day if he wanted to, and no one cared.

But finally Chipungu heard of a school that had been started off in the bush, and since he was a curious little boy and wanted to find out all he could about everything strange, he trotted off to see this strange thing which had been started.

Little Chipungu soon showed that he was made of stronger stuff than many other boys. For usually they started to learn but easily got tired and ran off to their cattle and goats and their strange games. But Chipungu was an industrious boy, and he stayed and learned to read and write, until he was considered to be a very wise boy by the villagers.

When a letter came to any village, the old ones sent for Chipungu so they could learn the message. Then they would get him to write the answer, so they could send it away. Oh, Chipungu was thought to be a very wise boy in those days. Later he became a Christian and was baptized, and he began to teach school.

Once he was teaching near the Mwami Mission station, near Fort Jameson in Northern Rhodesia. There are many mountains and caves around Mwami, so there are many wild beasts, too, which roam all around. Chipungu had to go about six miles to get to a place where he could buy salt or cloth or kerosene. Those journeys were made in the day-time, because it is safer to travel then.

One day Chipungu said to his wife, "I must go to the village around the mountain with the pastor today. There is a sick man there who has sent for us, and we want to take him some medicine. We will come back before it is dark."

"All right," said his wife. "But be sure to come back before night, for the villagers say the lions are getting worse these days."

"We are going on bicycles, so we can come back quickly," replied Chipungu; and away he went with the pastor, over the winding paths, through the trees and high grasses.

Chipungu's wife was a wise and good woman. However, she did not own any shoes or stockings or pretty dishes. Her house was made of mud with grass tied on in bunches for the roof. Here she "kept house," as African mothers do, and took care of her fat black babies as well as she could. Even though she was poor and did not know many things, she did know how to pray. So when she saw her husband ride away happily, she knelt down on the earthen floor and prayed. She knew that the bush was full of dangers, and that something might happen to her kind husband.

After Chipungu left his home, he and the pastor traveled down a road for a long time. A small number of people in the country have cars, so it is necessary for a few roads to be made, but they are bad ones indeed. They rode along side by side for several miles and talked about this and that until they had to turn off onto a tiny native footpath that ran alongside a high mountain.

"It is lucky it is daytime," shouted the pastor, who rode along behind. "The people all about here are troubled with lions!"

"Yes," said Chipungu. "But they are all hidden away now, I suppose. They sleep in the day and hunt at night."

The ground was smooth where they were riding and a bit downhill, so they could go fast. Just as Chipungu turned a sharp bend around a thick bush, he almost stopped breathing. In the path just ahead of him trotted four big lions.

He almost stopped breathing. In the path just ahead of him trotted four big lions.

What could he do? He was going too fast to stop, and if he hit the lions, he'd tumble off the bicycle, and then he'd surely be killed and eaten.

Suddenly his finger touched the bicycle bell. "Pr-r-r-r-r-ing! Pr-r-r-r-r-ing! Pr-r-r-r-r-ing!" It buzzed. Instantly the lions jumped to the side of the road, just as scared of the bell as Chipungu was of them. At that very instant the two bicycles flashed past the lions, so near to the great creatures that the man's legs brushed the tawny fur.

The pastor and Chipungu were so scared they were not able to talk for over an hour. When they went home, many men went with them carrying spears and knives. But they were safe the first time, for the angel of the Lord was encamping round about them.

You see, Chipungu's wife prayed and God heard her prayer.

Gerson and Damson and the Elephants

MOST boys and girls think that the lion, the leopard, and the crocodile are the fiercest beasts in Africa. But this is wrong. There are two other animals that are much more dangerous. One is the elephant, and the other is the wild buffalo. If you get either of them angry at you, you do not have much chance to get away. One day a female elephant became irritated at a man driving in a motorcar past her and her baby elephant. She ran after him, trumpeting angrily. With a mighty rush she slammed into the car, and over it went into the ditch. Luckily no one was hurt. The man stayed very still till the angry old mother went away. Then he crawled out quietly and got helpers to right the car before he went on his way.

But our story is about Gerson Mandula and Damson, his brother. One day they had almost fifty miles to walk after they got off the rickety old bus in Blantyre, Nyasaland. The first thing those black boys did was to take off their shoes, for Africans can walk much better barefoot. Then, too, shoes are costly in Africa, and the boys did not want to waste good shoe leather on the long journey.

As they went along, they sang some of the songs they had learned in school back at Malamulo. Hour after hour they walked. Finally, just before they got to the Shire River, they spied a "canteen," as they call the rough restaurants they have in the little mud houses.

Gerson and Damson stopped for a big dish of nourishing porridge. Afterward they went down by the bank of the Shire and soaked their tired feet for a little while. Then, drying them on grass, they went on their way.

That night the boys slept with their friends at Matandani Mission. They had a good game with the boys on the *bwalo* after supper, even though they were tired. Then they spread out their blankets and slept soundly.

The next morning Gerson and Damson started out early. Only seventeen miles more, and there would be dear mother, the small children and father, and a good supper waiting. The boys knew that their mother would stew a chicken and bake some little mealie cakes in the oven she had dug down in the ground. Then there would be roasted sweet potatoes, boiled eggplant, and all the sugar cane they could eat.

Soon they were climbing the high hill leading to the school near which their dear father lived.

"Let's cut across here," suggested Damson. "It's lots closer and we can get home sooner."

Gerson was the older, and he considered the matter a moment. He looked up at the sun. "It's early, and there isn't so much danger of wild beasts," he said. "It isn't going to rain, so the ridge path will be safe. Yes, let's go."

Off at a right angle from the main road went the little bush path winding in and out, over and around, up and down, and through dimpling little streams.

They fairly ran, they were so glad to be so near home. Damson, who was ahead, suddenly stopped short.

"Gerson," he said, "what is that coming down the road ahead? It looks like big gray stones. Maybe they rolled down the hillside. Oh-h-h-h-h, Gerson, they're elephants! Oh! Oh! Where shall we go?"

On one side was a deep chasm, and on the other, a cliff went straight up. The boys looked around wildly. Off behind them was a heap of gigantic rocks, just at the side of the chasm. The boys crept back and lay flat among the gray stones. They were trembling with fear. Then the big herd of elephants swept past, flapping their big ears and switching their tiny tails. Their small eyes looked wicked and cruel. In a few minutes five huge elephants thundered by. Luckily they did not see the two trembling black boys. If they had, Gerson and Damson would have been killed. But they were safe, and now they are back in school at old Malamulo. They don't care if they *never* see another elephant.

"Gerson," said Damson, "what is that coming down the road ahead? It looks like big gray stones."

Wedson

HE IS a cook, just a humble cook for the unmarried women workers at their big house at Malamulo Mission. You see, all these women are so busy and their work is so constant that they need someone to look after their kitchen and wash dishes.

There is Miss Mary Ford, who is head nurse at the Malamulo Hospital. Her duties are so many that she can only rush home and eat, then rush away again. There's a school for nurses and orderlies going on all the time, besides the dozens of patients to care for. Her home is in Wales, but she is so busy she just hardly has time to think of the green valleys and the skylarks and the flowers in her beautiful little country.

Miss Muriel Howe is a nurse, too, a dynamic, energetic little woman, who came from Australia. She spent many years in China before she had to leave because of the Russian occupation.

Miss Margaret Johnson lives at the single workers' house, too. She has given many years of her life to the lepers who live in the hundreds of small houses in the Malamulo Leper Colony. Every spare moment is spent making the colony into a bower of beauty. The flowers there are so beautiful that one almost forgets that those who live there are victims of the "living death."

Then there is Miss Ruth Foote, who for many years took care of the girls' and women's work at Malamulo, which reached a high level of efficiency during her years of painstaking, unselfish supervision. Her work keeps her busy from dawn until dark. How could she cook? So Wedson prepares pies, cakes, and roasts, boils beans and spinach, and mashes the potatoes. He works hard and does all he can to please.

But if you'll look close, you'll notice that he can't quite open one eye. The other eye is so wide open it looks as if he might spill it out of its socket. He looks very queer, poor soul. Why? Well, I will tell you.

One day, when I first came to Malamulo, I heard a large crowd of people bellowing and shouting and screaming as they came down the mission path. I ran out of my house and followed them to the hospital. They were carrying Wedson in a hammock. But, oh, his face! his face! I gave him one glance; then I had to look away. It was so terrible. Have you ever looked into the window of a butcher shop and seen raw beefsteak lying on big white trays ready to sell? That is the way poor Wedson's face looked. His eyes looked as though they were both torn out. I turned to run away, for it makes me sick to see such terrible sights, when I almost jumped out of my shoes. There on the ground beside me lay a dead leopard. His head was beaten to a pulp. Here is what happened:

Wedson had gone hunting that day. He had hoped to find a little buck or a guinea fowl or two. He had arrows and a bow, a knobkerrie stick, and his faithful dog.

They had gone far into the bush when the dog gave a peculiar yipping howl that ended almost in a sob. Wedson turned to look at the dog, and when he turned his head, he

Ten yards away, half concealed by a clump of rough
bushes, was the crouching form of this big leopard.

saw the danger. Ten yards away, half concealed by a clump
of rough bushes, was the crouching form of this big leopard.
His amber eyes glared hungrily. Six feet from them was the
tip of the tail lashing angrily. His hindquarters rocked with
the motion of the cat tribe, preliminary to leaping.

Then before Wedson could collect his wits, he saw a dim
streak in the air and felt a frightful blinding, flashing pain
on his face as if ten thousand live coals were cutting into
his flesh and eyes.

He felt himself blindly thrashing with his knobkerrie; he
felt it hitting, hitting. Horrible snarls told Wedson that his
dog was helping.

Crash, crash, went the knobkerrie. Through the curtain

53

of streaming blood he tried to see that every blow told. When the leopard fell, he did too. The next thing he knew, he was in a machila on his way to Malamulo, carried there by friendly villagers.

The leopard went, too, only it was too late for him. He is now a beautiful rug. Wedson, the cook, will bear the marks of his terrific fight with the leopard all his life.

Wopha Mikango

WHEN you stand high up on one of the mountains of the Shire Highlands, you can look down into the Dambo, as the Shire River Valley is called. It is green and lovely, and the river curls through it like a beautiful gray satin ribbon. You think, "Oh, I would be so happy if I could get down there in that beautiful place." But when you get there, you want to get out, if you can, for it is not so pleasant as it looks.

There are great rice fields, with millions of malaria mosquitoes rising from the wet valley every night. They fill the blood of the Dambo dwellers with the germs that bring terrible malaria, with its chills, fever, vomiting, and often death.

Then, lurking in the dense bush and around the rocky hills are many beasts. The lion, the leopard, and the cowardly hyena are all there, waiting to go forth at night and kill the goats, cattle, and fowls of the poor valley dwellers. As a consequence the people build kraals into which they drive their animals at night. These are made by planting certain types of saplings close together, and they often begin growing right away. They make a fine fence, all leafed out and living and growing.

But lions can jump over kraals easily, kill a cow or two, and have a splendid feast before morning. The people hear the fearful roars, but they are much too afraid to leave their homes to rescue their animals. So they just stay inside their mud huts and tremble and tremble.

Lions had been killing many cattle in the villages near Winfred's home. He was herdboy for his father's cattle, and he grew to know the sleek, fat humpbacked beasts, and he loved them very much.

One night he called a meeting of all his friends in the village.

"Who is brave?" he cried. "Who is not afraid to sleep with me in the village kraal tonight? Then if the lions come, we will shout loudly and scare them away and save our fathers' cattle! Our names will be great in the village tomorrow if we do this thing!"

Four sturdy black boys stepped forward.

"We will sleep with you in the kraal tonight," they promised with a great show of bravery.

"Then bring your spears and plenty of stones, at least a basketful apiece," said Winfred. "Be here at sunset with your blankets."

The boys fixed up a sleeping place for themselves at the side of the kraal. They had brought three of their home-made beds, some mats to cover them, and some bamboos to shelter them a little from the steaming flanks of the big, lumbering beasts.

I think I would have had a sleepless night there in that kraal because of the strong smells, the dirt, and the hard-biting insects. Winfred and his friends were not worried a bit. They had smelled strong smells before, and dirt was little thought of; as for the small biting creatures, the boys were concerned more with big biting ones.

So wrapped in smelly, poorly washed harsh blankets, wearing the furiously dirty rags they had worn for many days, five boys lay down to sleep in a cattle kraal that stank to high heaven. They all went to sleep almost as soon as they had touched the mats spread across the rickety bedsteads.

Sometime in the night—they had no way to know when, for none owned either clock or watch—they were awakened by the cattle milling about nervously and letting out plaintive, frightened cries.

Sleep still dragged down their weary eyelids, when suddenly a terrible roar made them all sit up at once. Instantly the cattle crammed as close to the boys as they could get, crying out in almost human voices. All around the beds was a solid wall of trembling cattle flesh. Death was very near and they knew it.

Then, in the bright moonlight, they saw the form of a huge lion flash over their heads right into the kraal. His body was only inches from their heads. With a mighty sweep of his great paw, the lion slashed at a young bull. Soon he lay bleeding and uttering little bleating cries of pain and terror. The boys could hardly move for fear.

Suddenly Winfred seized his spear. The lion was facing the other way, working busily on the neck of the young victim. The boy raised the long, razor-sharp blade. With all his young strength he hurled it at the huge cat, fell over backward, and crept under the beds. His companions were there before him, shaking like leaves.

The lion gave one terrible roar; then they heard no sounds for quite some time except the cries and moans of the frightened cattle. Then there was silence—far more fearful and frightening than the noise had been.

At last Winfred ventured to peep out. The cattle were

Winfred seized his spear. The lion was facing the other way, working busily on the neck of the young victim.

standing still. Already they seemed to have stupidly forgotten their danger. Some were even swinging their jaws in their business of cud chewing.

Slowly, cautiously, Winfred crept out. Fearfully he peered over the bunched black backs of the cattle. There, sprawled in the middle of the kraal, lay two dead creatures: a young bull, his neck broken by the fierce blow of the lion, and the lion himself, with Winfred's spear sticking into his great chest.

With a glad cry Winfred leaped high in the air. Then his companions crept out. Brave now. Brave enough.

"*Tapha Mkango!*" cried one of them joyously.

"We? We?" questioned Winfred. "No, no, boys! *Iai! Iai! Ndapha mkango.* Not *we,* but *I* killed this lion!"

Can you see why the village people called that boy *Wopha Mikango* (Lion Killer) after that?

Only Three Shillings

IN THE years gone by, the African people had only one way of getting any place. That was walking. There were no roads before the white men came and opened up the country. Also, there were many, many wild beasts and snakes ready to hurt or kill the natives if they went out into the bush very far. So most of the Africans never wandered very far from their native villages in those dark, terrible days.

Naturally when roads began to be cut through the wilderness, and a few trucks and automobiles came into the country, these ignorant people were very much afraid. Some of them thought that cars were big beasts coming to devour them, and they ran away into the bush as fast as their trembling legs could carry them.

After a while they learned that cars and trucks would not hurt them. The natives called them *galimoto,* and they are called that to this very day. Nowadays Africans love to ride in *galimoto.* They are amazed that they can go so fast and can get so far in a single day. So every chance they get, they will ride in the back of big rough trucks.

Wilson is the son of a man named Menyere, who lives in a village named Thambani. He wanted so much to ride home from Blantyre in the *galimoto*. It was almost a hundred miles to walk, and it would take him several days on foot. In the *galimoto* he could get there in one day and by nightfall could be eating with his family.

But the truck driver got three shillings from everyone who rode, and Wilson did not have that much money. So the poor boy saw some of his friends climbing high on top of the maize bags and getting set for the journey. Then he gathered his little bundle and started out on the long, weary walk.

The truck bounced past him and disappeared in a cloud of dust down the bumpy road. That evening the boy slept at Chileka Mission, which is just fifteen miles from Blantyre. The next morning one of the mothers boiled him some corn so he could have a little lunch when he got hungry at noon. So away he went again—walking, walking, walking, over the harsh, hot road till his feet burned like coals of fire

All the time he kept thinking of his companions who must be home by now, and there he was, still trudging along wearily. A little after noon he came to a bend in the road. Just around the turn he saw many people looking at something by the side of the road and talking excitedly.

"What is it?" he cried, breaking into a run.

"This is a bad wreck," one man replied. "Yesterday a wheel came off this big *galimoto*, and it turned over and rolled down this hill. Then it began to burn. Six people were killed. Five of them were Africans."

Wilson stood there and looked at the twisted iron and smoke-blackened wreck that used to be a *galimoto*. If he had had three shillings, where would he be?

Suddenly he began to cry, and he started out walking on toward home. For once in his life he was thankful he was a poor boy.

Filemon

AFTER the boy Filemon had had his terrible adventure with the great python, he still did not know very much about civilization or God. He thought that death and sickness were caused by bewitching. He thought that it was necessary to chase the evil spirits out of the garden before any seed should be planted.

He believed in offering the first fruits of the garden to the spirits to appease their anger. Then, because he lived among these heathen people, he became fond of doing what they did. Whenever he saw anyone drinking beer, he would run quickly so he could get a drink of the beer, too.

Often he walked several miles to attend beer dances. When he heard the boom, boom, boom of the drums, away he ran with his friends to dance and to drink, sometimes all night long. At times bad things happened at these beer dances. One night a man got angry at another man, took a knife, and cut him so badly that he died that very night. Of course the people ran home right away, for they were afraid of the police. Filemon did not realize that it was the beer which made the people do dreadful things like that.

Then he became fond of tobacco. He liked to make little cigarettes and smoke them all day. He liked to chew tobacco. He liked it when his saliva became an ugly dirty brown. You see, Filemon had never learned that God does not like us to spoil our bodies with the dirty and hurtful things of this world.

One day Filemon received an invitation to visit an old friend in a distant village. Filemon had gone to many dances with this boy, and he naturally thought they would drink and smoke and dance all the week end. He arrived at his friend's house just at sunset Friday night. He was all ready and eager for a good time.

He heard singing coming from inside the house. Stepping to the door, he looked in. The whole family were sitting on mats, and they were singing. They were all washed and clean. What was all this? Then the father called him.

"Come, sit down, my boy. We are now *Akristu*, and we do not follow after the evil ways of the heathen any more."

Filemon was puzzled and surprised when he sat down on the mat by his friend. The songs sounded beautiful, so he tried hard to learn them.

Just as you sing songs you love, Filemon learned to sing one that night. He especially enjoyed one song. While *you* sing:

> "Is my name written there,
> On the page white and fair?
> In the book of Thy kingdom,
> Is my name written there?"

He learned to sing:

> *"Kodi mwalembamo*
> *Dzina langalotu*
> *M'buku la kumwambako*
> *Kodi mwalembamo?"*

Just then the mother called them to come eat. In the center of the table was a great snow-white mound of *nsima* made from fine corn meal. Then in another dish was *ndiwo* made of onions, cabbage, and tomatoes. After the father had prayed over the food, they all took turns pinching pieces off the *nsima*. Then, after they had made the little pieces into little balls, they dipped them into the rich *ndiwo* and popped them into their mouths. It was very good indeed, and Filemon ate a great deal, for his journey had made him hungry.

The mother had a basket of roasted sweet potatoes and some good ripe bananas, so Filemon felt he was full when he got ready to lie down with his friend on the mat. Then he asked his friend the question that had troubled him all evening.

"What did that song mean, Dzino, where it said about writing down my name?"

"Why, Filemon, that means to become *Akristu*. When we promise to follow *Yesu Kristu,* then we know our names are written down in the book of God up in heaven."

"How do you follow *Yesu Kristo,* Dzino? I would like for my name to be written down in God's book."

"Then, Filemon, you can't follow the drums for dancing and drinking beer any more. You can't swear or eat or burn the tobacco. You have to leave off all those things of this world."

Filemon then thought of the dances, of the anger, quarrels, and fights which had ended a time or two with murder. The police had come to the village several times for such dreadful "cases."

Suddenly he could see plainly that the beer, tobacco, and the dances were of no value. He knew that mothers neglected their little children when they were drunk. He knew that fathers wasted much of the money of the poor family at such times.

Because Filemon had a good heart, he prepared it to serve the Lord. Now he is one of the *Akristu,* and this is what he says: "I want my poor family to find Christ, too. I want my father, mother, and sisters and brothers to be happy in the beautiful city Jesus is preparing for us."

Let us pray that Filemon may be successful in winning them from heathenism.

The Boy Who Promoted Himself Backward

THE KARONGA district of northern Nyasaland is a big and needy place. It has many, many villages where the name of Christ is never heard. Many of the heathen count all their wealth in cattle. The little boys of the family are sent to herd these cattle, so thousands of them never see the inside of a schoolroom. Kaonga wanted to go to school very much, but his heathen father thought it was foolishness and told him that he must herd his cattle.

Then Kaonga entered into a little bargain with his friends whereby they would herd his cattle at least three days of the week. With that, ragged little Kaonga trudged several miles to Nthalire village to attend school in a miserable little mud building. He had to sit on the mud floor, and he learned to write in mud with a sharp stick. Even with his three days a week, he got along faster than the lazy children who came every day. In this way he went through grades one, two, three, four, and five.

When one gets to grade six, he has to go to a certain kind of school called a station school. At last Kaonga's father consented to let him go eighty miles away to attend this station school for grade six. The boy was glad.

Kaonga started out happily on his long journey. He had

hardly anything to carry, for he did not own a thing but the pitiful rags on his back. He had a rough blanket his mother had made from the bark of a tree. It was called *nkhwende* and was strong, but it smelled bad and was scratchy. Poor Kaonga did not worry so much about that, for he had been "itchy" all his life. Unless he kept his hair short, it got full of lice. He was bitten every day and every night by mosquitoes, ticks, flies, jigger fleas, bedbugs, or cockroaches.

At last, after traveling three hot, weary days, he was glad to see the mission road leading off through the bush. How his heart leaped with joy! In an hour he could be all established with the other boys, ready to begin learning grade six. He followed the rocky grass-grown road joyously. He was dirty, he was ragged, and he was hungry. But what did that matter? Soon he would be a student and on his way to a good education.

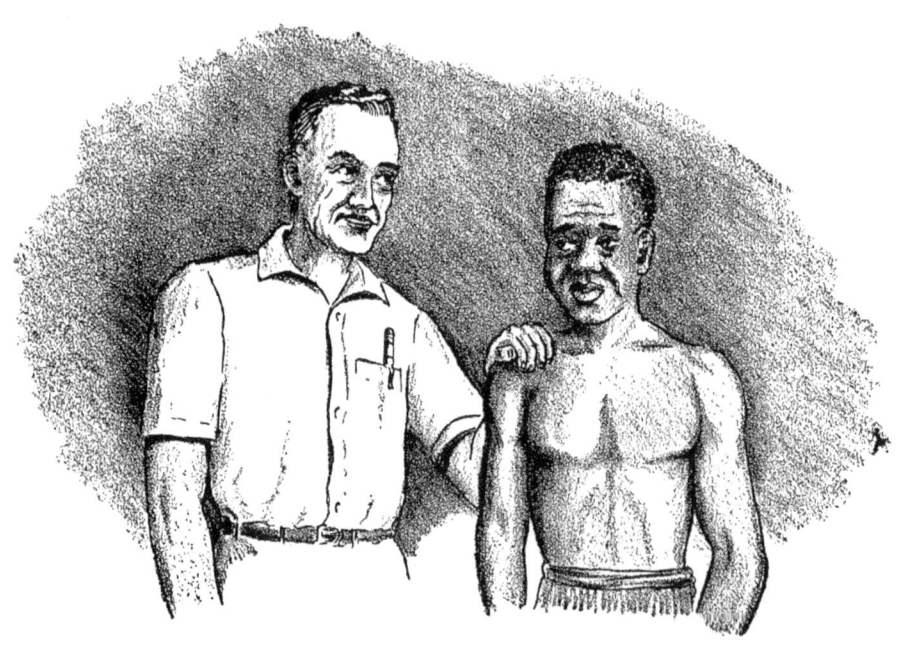

When he presented himself to the director, he heard the bad news directly.

But a sad disappointment awaited Kaonga. Even though he had arrived several days early, the place was full to over-flowing with boys of every size. When he presented himself to the director, he heard the bad news directly.

"Hard luck, my boy! I am sorry!" the kind man said. "But there's not a bit of room left. Come back next year!"

Kaonga couldn't understand it then, but he soon did. He was still a heathen boy and did not know about the true God. When he got back to his village three days later, his father was sorry for the boy. "Kaonga," he said, to comfort him, "there is a school of *Akristu* in the village six miles away. Your uncle lives there. Go stay with him and learn, my boy."

The next morning Kaonga started out on blistered feet for the village school. When he got there, he found out that only grades one and two were being taught.

He was discouraged, but he stayed right there and took the second grade again. The teacher was a Christian, and he lent the big boy his Bible to read. He read and read and read. It was not long until he began to learn how lovely Jesus our Saviour is. And after many wonderful conversations with the good Christian teacher, he began to long to be *Akristu,* too.

Today Kaonga is a Christian; he has been for several years. He is now working on the Teacher Training Course, so he can go back to the Karonga and show his people the glorious light of God.

He is poor, very poor, blind in one eye, and is all alone in his beliefs; but he has a great ambition to lead his people out of the slavery of sin just as Moses led the children of Israel out of Egypt long ago. And he will, too. You will see him someday in heaven, if you are good enough to get there, too.

The New Trousers

I AM sure that you all have been happy at some time over something that mother has bought for you. It may have been a new pink dress, a pair of shiny shoes, or some long trousers. But even so, before you got the new thing, you probably had plenty of others tucked away in your dresser drawers.

Katundu had one thing to wear. It was a piece of banana leaf which had been heated near the fire so it would not tear. This was fastened to his waist by a homemade string made out of the bark of a certain tree.

He was about nine years old, and he had never owned a thread of any kind of cloth in his whole life. Just that little breech cloth of banana leaf—that was all he had to cover his small black body. It was hot where Katundu lived, so he did not suffer from the cold, except when icy rains sluiced down day and night for weeks. Then he trembled with the cold.

Long before that, when Katundu was a baby, his big brother Mtegha had gone down into South Africa to the big city of Johannesburg to work in the gold mines. Nothing had been heard of him for all these years. Mtegha could not write; neither could the parents. So how could he send any word to his home? It was as if he had died and was put in the grave.

One glad day while Katundu was playing in the bush with some of his friends, they heard talking. They saw a man dressed in good clothes approaching, pushing a beautiful bicycle. Behind him came three carriers, bringing big boxes covered with checkered linoleum such as the Africans like to buy for trunks in Johannesburg.

"Who is this great one?" whispered Katundu to the boys who were with him.

"We cannot tell," answered one. "But say! His face is like the face of your father, Katundu! It is as if he is the twin brother!"

Then Katundu had a happy thought. Could this be Mtegha, the brother who had long ago disappeared into the south? Could it be he? Fearfully he stepped forward.

"Mtegha?" he whispered.

The great one swung around quickly and looked at the little black boy. The child's round eyes looked wonderingly up into the man's face.

"Who are you?" the big one demanded. "How did you know I am Mtegha?"

"I am Katundu, son of Mbalebale," he piped. "Your face looks like the face of Mbalebale, my father. Mtegha, my brother, went away long, long ago. I wondered, I thought—" Here Katundu stopped open-mouthed, for the stranger had laid the beautiful bicycle down and had picked him up in his arms joyfully.

"Mbale wanga!" he cried. *"Mbale wanga!"* Even though Mtegha had lived among those who spoke a strange language for eight years, he still had not forgotten how to say "my brother" in his beloved tongue.

Then such gabble and babble and joy when they arrived

together at the little mud hut that was home! The old mother and father wept aloud and clapped their hands for joy. They had never hoped to see the face of their first-born son again. The father sent a boy quickly to kill a goat, a rooster, and a fat hen, and another boy was sent to the store to buy some sugar. Rice had been harvested, so it was soon put to cooking in black earthen pots in the kitchen house.

Such buzzing activity! Water was heated in big pots, so Mtegha could cleanse the dust of travel from his body. Then when the family gathered around the great mound of white flaky rice and the pot of chicken and cooked goat, there was much joy and laughter.

Afterward Mtegha opened up the boxes he had brought with him from far-off Johannesburg. Never had such an array of strange things been seen in that primitive village. Katundu was so excited that his legs itched. A great fluffy blanket was laid out for mother, and two strong shirts and a pair of great shoes were for father, who never had had a shoe on his tough, irony feet in all his days.

For brother Chule was a shirt and strong trousers to re-place the cloth he had wrapped about his lean loins. For sister Manesti were some glass beads, some bangles for both her arms and her legs, and a bright-red calico dress. But even while Katundu was admiring the lovely things of others, Mtegha lifted a bright little red shirt and some blue trousers from the trunk.

"These are for you, Katundu."

"Ine, Ine!" cried Katundu, taking the gorgeous things in his small hands. Then he looked down at the banana leaf, the only clothing his small body had ever known.

"But you must help me to wear them," he cried out ex-citedly. "Me, I do not know how to put them on!"

So Katundu put clothing on his small
body for the first time in his life.

So Katundu put clothing on his small body for the first time in his life. Then Mtegha put some money in the little pockets.

"These are for school fees," he said joyfully. "You, little brother, must go to school and learn. Who knows but that you may be a great man someday?"

Because of Mtegha's interest Katundu started to go to school, the first one in his whole family to do such a thing. Even after Mtegha left and went back to Johannesburg, money and clothing came from time to time to help the little boy. But one day a letter came to the village addressed to Katundu Mbalebale. In it was the sad news that brother Mtegha was dead.

"There was a fearful accident in the mines," wrote a

friend. "I am sorry to tell you that your brother Mtegha is dead."

Katundu is a young man today, graduating from the teacher's course. He has had other shirts and pairs of trousers since that day long ago, but he counts those first ones the best of all. It was because he had never owned any other clothing before in all his life.

He Played Dead

WHEN Teacher Nelias Casweha was a little boy, he had a great and terrible adventure with a leopard. He escaped only because he had listened to the counsel of his old grandfather.

"If a leopard or a lion is chasing you, my boy," the old man said, "do not run. You see, they are like big cats, and cats chase moving things. Lie still and pretend that you are dead. It is very likely that your life will be saved if you do this."

Nelias had said then and there that he would do that thing if he ever had an adventure with a wild animal in the forest.

One bright day Nelias and four other boys started out with five dogs, some clubs and spears, bows and arrows, for a big hunt in the bush. If they had known what was to happen that day, I am sure not a one would have left his house. But none of us knows from one day to another what will happen to us. So these five African boys could not have known.

The day went by quickly. The boys caught several small animals and fowls, but still they were not satisfied.

"We want a buck or a *mpalampala* at least," the oldest

one said. So they went farther and farther into the dense bush.

Suddenly, as if in answer to the expressed desire, a beautiful deer sprang nimbly out of a clump of rough bushes. Instantly the dogs were upon the beautiful creature and bore her to the ground. The boys were elated.

"Let us try to get another," one of them shouted.

"No, I think we ought to go home," objected Nelias. "It is getting late. See? The sun is low."

"Nelias is a girl and afraid of the dark!" jeered the other boys. "Are you coming with us, or are you going home to ride on your mother's back?"

Reluctantly he went on with his companions. He knew it was not safe, though, for he knew that the beasts go forth at the waning of the sun to search for their food. It was at this hour he always heard the roar of the lion.

The dogs had run on ahead, yipping and yapping excitedly. Suddenly they entered another patch of bush. Then a terrible uproar arose—so fearful that Nelias felt his whole scalp prickle and his hair stand right up on his head. The dogs all seemed to be yelping at once. The bush was crashing, and a fearsome growling filled the air. Then all was still.

The boys looked at one another.

"Are the dogs dead?" one whispered.

"What is it?" asked another.

"Let us run!" suggested a third.

Nelias, remembering the counsel of his grandfather, crept behind a bush and lay very still. His companions turned to run, but as they did, a yellow streak of fury darted from the clump of bushes.

Nelias heard the screams of his friends, but he lay still. At last he crept quietly back to the village and told the

Nelias, remembering the counsel of his grandfather, crept behind a bush and lay very still.

people that they should go and hunt for those boys. With
flaming torches every man in the village went forth.

Nelias heard the mournful death wails when they returned about an hour and a half later. All his companions
were dead. Nelias alone was saved.

The Boy Who Whipped a Leopard

NYERENDA was a small boy who lived in a bush village far from civilization. Even though there is one train track which goes through Nyasaland, there are hundreds and thousands of people who never have seen a train in their lives. They also think that thunder is made by a big bird, and that evil spirits cause drouths and floods.

Nyerenda's father had many cattle and goats. Up in that poor northern Nyasaland village wealth is measured by the number of cattle a man possesses. The people do not consider that schools are worth anything, so they just send their boys out to herd cattle instead. This practice causes a great deal of trouble; the boys hate and despise their parents when they get older, for they see that the parents have deprived them of a good chance in life. So little Nyerenda was sent out to the bush to care for cattle instead of to go to school.

One day he was herding cattle on a grassy hillside near the village. He was sitting on a stone whistling gaily and throwing stones at some birds in a nearby tree. Suddenly a great uproar arose among the cattle. The whole herd ran toward Nyerenda, small that he was, as if they thought he could do something to protect them.

"What is the matter? What is the matter?" he cried out,

standing on the stone, stretching to see what the cause of the commotion was. Over on the far side of the herd he saw what looked like one of the big bulls chewing and fighting another young bull.

"Stop! Stop!" he screamed, seizing his knobkerrie and running toward the fight. Would he have screamed like that if he had known it was a leopard that had attacked the young bull?

Well, he did not know, so with great anger in his young heart he ran right up to the leopard and began beating it over the head with his knobkerrie. He hit it with all the might of his young arms.

Luckily his father had been nearby in his garden and heard the attack at the same time that Nyerenda did, so he was near at hand, armed with a sharp spear.

Just then the leopard gave a terrible snarl and leaped on the boy and knocked him violently to the ground. He would certainly have died then and there if Nyerenda's father had not run a spear through the leopard's heart.

So little Nyerenda was saved. But he refused to go to the bush any more to herd cattle. His father saw nothing else to do but send him to school. Thus a leopard was the cause of Nyerenda's getting an education. Wasn't that strange?

The Lion That Jumped Over the Moon

NOT FAR from Nyasaland is a great territory belonging to Portugal. This country is called Portuguese East Africa, or Mozambique. There are many, many wild beasts in this country, because it is not settled so much as Nyasaland. Towns are much farther apart, too, and there are fewer people.

It sometimes happens that hunters from Nyasaland like to go over into that country to try to catch some game. One day a boy named Witman decided to go to Portuguese East Africa to hunt. He did not have a gun, but he did have a strong bow and many sharp arrows. His friend Matimati had an old gun, so the two went to catch some game. If they killed a leopard, the skin could easily be sold for two pounds sterling; and if they killed a deer, the meat would bring quite a bit of money if they took it to the villages. Happy and full of life, they started out.

Witman was a student at Malamulo Mission, and he was eager to earn some money for clothes and school fees. They talked eagerly as they walked the long distance to the hunting ground, each telling the other what he was going to do with the money.

Their destination for that day was the home of Matimati's

brother. There they intended to sleep for the night, then press on farther to a place where hunting was said to be very good. But when they arrived at the village, everyone was excited. A lion had gotten into the herd that afternoon and had killed a young heifer.

"It is certain to return for more tonight, so we men are all going to sleep in the kraal with the cattle. If we shout loud enough, we can scare it away," said the brother.

"I'll sleep there with you," agreed Matimati, "and so will Witman. Surely we will scare the old fellow, and perhaps we can kill him."

Witman was not what you would say enthusiastic over his prospective night in a cattle kraal. In making a kraal, the natives first dig a great circular trench. Into this trench, side by side, they put limbs and branches about four to six inches in diameter. Most of them start to grow in time, so there is soon a thick fence all around the cattle kraal. Inside, the manure gets to be about two feet deep and smells terrible. Fleas and ticks are everywhere.

To Witman's eyes the horns of the big humpbacked creatures looked sharp indeed. But Matimati had spoken, and he had to do as he was bidden or be called a coward. After eating supper, they all sat around the fire and told tales that almost curdled Witman's blood.

One old fellow in particular seemed to take delight in scaring the daylights out of everyone. "Right here in this very kraal my own grandpa was killed by lions," he stated, complacently puffing at his pipe. "He heard the cattle in a commotion and went out."

He puffed his pipe for a while.

"He didn't come back," he added slyly, looking sidewise at the trembling boys.

"Right here?" queried Witman in a scared voice.

"Right here in this very kraal my own grandpa was killed by lions," he stated, complacently puffing at his pipe.

"Right on this spot," asserted the old man positively. "I tell you, the lions—the leopards even—they are bad around here. As for me, I won't sleep in no kraal tonight. I don't want a lion gnawing on my old bones!"

By that time Witman wished heartily he was back in his own village near Malamulo. So populous and well settled was his home area that leopards came only occasionally, and sometimes a year or two would pass before a lion would be heard of. At last the fire died down, and some rough beds were carried to the kraal. Matimati and Witman were to sleep on one small bed.

Witman, with his blanket roll, crept gingerly into the sticky place and lay down at the foot of the slatted bed, occupied already by the snoring Matimati. Lying there wide awake and quaking with fear, Witman wondered what the night would bring forth. The great full moon sank lower and lower, till it seemed almost as if it were peeping over the rough kraal fence. Suddenly the cattle began to mill about and push against his bed. In the moonlight Witman could see the rolling whites of their eyes.

Then the form of a huge lion hurtled right over the low kraal fence. To Witman it seemed as if he had really jumped over the moon. Simultaneous with the leap, the frightened lad heard the crack of a rifle, and the great beast fell to the ground—dead.

When the boys finally got out of the kraal, they saw the old grandfather, clad in only a loincloth, calmly reloading his old-fashioned rifle.

"Heh, heh," he chuckled. "I got him that time." Then he laughed for a long time. "Mighta been the grandson of the one that killed my old grandpa," he remarked wisely.

The Wild Buffalo

SOMEONE once told me of a certain kind of whip called a *chikoti* made out of buffalo skin. I did not think much about it until I saw a piece of buffalo skin. Then it scared me.

"What! Do they whip people with that?" I asked.

"Yes, yes," came the answer. "Many slaves have died under the *chikoti*."

The buffalo as seen here in Africa is a fierce and terrible animal. To meet one is almost certain death. But around the southern part of Nyasaland there are very few buffaloes, for the white man's gun has thinned them out until there is just one or two seen now and then.

Nickers Chinsinya was a little black boy who lived near a place called Cileka. He had never seen a buffalo in his life, though he had heard the older ones talking about them and telling what fearful creatures they were. For around the blazing fires at night, these people sat and told stories of the fearful events of the olden days.

The day was bright and shining, and all over the level land men, women, and children were bending over the land hoeing. Nickers straightened up to rest his tired back, when he spied a fierce creature running up from the woods with

He spied a fierce creature running up
from the woods with terrific speed.

terrific speed. His great head was lowered, and flecks of foaming saliva slathered from his ugly mouth.

"Amai, Bambo!" he shrieked, anxious to warn his father and mother, who were near him.

They saw the creature in time to run away with their boy, but others were not saved. Nickers saw one old man, grandfather Kamtoko, crushed right into the earth with the beast's ugly hoofs. A mother and her small baby were the next victims. Death spread all over those peaceful mealie lands.

Someone ran and brought help from the nearby police station. An *askari* came with a gun. Cautiously he approached the place where the creature was snorting and pawing the earth in anger. A bullet brought the murderer down. The creature was cut up, and the meat was divided among those who were hurt or who had relatives killed.

Koko

ONE DAY my cook boy, Sandula, and my house-boy, Cosalawa, began calling to me very urgently. "Dona, Dona, come here quickly!"

I dropped what I was doing and ran to the back door. What was it—a snake, a hawk, a giant chameleon? Chameleons are harmless, but the natives are traditionally afraid of them and would not touch them for anything.

Arriving at the kitchen door, I was confronted by Koko. She was the first baboon I ever saw close at hand or touched. Her little body was no bigger than my clenched fist, but her arms and legs were hairy and long, and her tail was of prodigious length.

At that time the Cinyanja language was just a jargon of queer unintelligible sounds, for I had been in Nyasaland for only six months when Koko came into my life. Yet some way these men who brought Koko to my door let me know that she was mine for the munificent sum of half a crown. That is about thirty-five or forty cents in United States money.

Poor little Koko thought that she had not a friend in all the world. The mother had been shot by an arrow as the little creature clung to her, and the sharp point of the arrow had passed through Koko's tiny hand before it pierced her mother's heart.

Her teeth were not yet strong enough for solid food, for she could not have been over a week old. It had been a day or two since she had eaten, and she was famished in her little baby way. Her tiny stomach caved in below her ribs.

Slowly I went over to claim my property, for the half crown had already been pocketed by the grinning hunter. Even more slowly I plucked her off the hunter's leg, for I was a little bit afraid of the needlelike teeth and the long fingernails. I took her up slowly, for I wanted to make her know that whatever scared her before need not worry her any more.

It seemed that she wanted above all things to have something to wrap her long arms and legs around, so I put her on my leg. She seized it with a deathlike grip, and I took her into the kitchen. Then I busied myself preparing a cup of warm sweetened milk for the tiny creature. Next I got an old bathroom rug and spread it on my lap. I set the cup on the table while I gently disengaged Koko from my ankle. She rebelled mightily at first, saying, "Ah-h-h-h-h, ah-h-h-h-h, ah-h-h-h-h," loudly while she tried to cling with all her tiny strength to my leg.

It seemed to be the only solid thing in her little life at that time. But as soon as that spoonful of warm milk touched her little tongue, it was a different matter entirely. She seized the spoon with such a firm grip that I could not get it to put back into the cup to get more milk, so I had to take another spoon and keep the first one filled. She sucked the milk with great glee.

Soon her little tummy was as round as a bowlful of jelly. Her eyes were drooping, and I knew she was almost ready to fall asleep. I washed her hands and whiskery little chin and put medicine on the wound. Then I wrapped her in a large towel and rocked her to sleep.

She looked pitiful with her tiny head nestled in the crook of my arm and one hand clutching a big button on the front of my dress for fear I would get away. From that hour she was mine—all mine. I laid her, towel and all, down on the warm hearth by the fireplace so she could sleep, and then I went about my work.

In about two hours I heard the breathy, "Ah-h-h-h-h-h-h, ah-h-h-h-h-h-h, ah-h-h-h-h-h-h." And I felt her arms and legs seizing my leg again. Again the cup and spoon performance went on, and again her stomach became as round as if she had swallowed a croquet ball.

For weeks I did all my work and gardening with a baby baboon wrapped around the calf of my leg. Koko was growing into baboon childhood. We became great friends. It was not long until she could eat peanuts and bananas; these became her favorite foods.

Koko had an immense capacity for affection. She loved me with all her heart. She was puzzled and sad when school began and she had to stay at home in the kitchen with Sandula or go out into the yard and play at her own little baboon games. Her presence at the school was not valued as she would have liked. Once she followed me there, but she grew tired of the long session and entered the room to see what the delay was. She leaped from one student's head to another's and created quite a commotion before she was caught, spanked, and put outside.

Her games in my yard consisted of removing the tails from as many of my chickens as she could catch. Bedlam reigned whenever she entered the hen yard. The chickens squawked and ran everywhere, hither and thither, but there was no escape. I had to spank her several times.

She liked to help me gather the eggs, but her services in that line were not highly valued either. I preferred to break my eggs into bowls in the house rather than to do things Koko's way. As it was, the grass between the hen house and the kitchen was one vast omelet.

Whenever I returned home, all I had to do was call out, "Koko, Koko." Even from a long distance I could hear her loud, breathy "Ah-h-h-h, ah-h-h-h, ah-h-h-h." I would hear a screen door go slam-bang, and soon she'd come, lickety-split down the path in the peculiar rabbitlike, kangaroolike lope of the baboon.

A baboon's tail sticks straight out from the body for possibly six inches, then it hangs down vertically almost at a right angle. As soon as she reached me when I called her, she would commandeer my leg, wrap arms, legs, and that queer tail around it, and hitchhike home. I liked her little habits. Koko was a delightful little pet.

I never saw anyone who had a look so pleading, so anguished, and so filled with love as did Koko when she spied me after I had gone the long journey into Blantyre to do my shopping. No one saw the car turn into the mission driveway as quick as she did. She was the first to greet me and was the most lavish in her endearments.

Daddy Lee, my husband's stepfather, is a beloved fixture in our household. After a while Koko decided that Daddy Lee was a fine substitute when I was not at home. So as he sat for long hours in the shade of the wide, cool porch, he had three loving companions: Koko, first and foremost and mistress of all situations; Spottie, the amiable, fierce-when-necessary rat terrier; and Mitzi, the purring pussycat.

Koko had several chores which she took care of faithfully every day. She carefully went through my hair every day from the vantage point of my right shoulder; she searched painstakingly through Daddy Lee's gray thatch too. She had at least one jealous fight with Spottie every day, no holds barred. Decision—a draw. She put Mitzi in her place several times a day. She removed all burrs, black jacks, and suchlike from Daddy Lee's and my clothing every day. She made mad passes at the chickens, climbed trees and tore up crows' nests, caught grasshoppers, and ate a prodigious number of bananas.

If Koko had taken the place on Daddy Lee's lap, or even on my lap if I got to sit down for a while, Spottie and Mitzi were sure to appear soon. Then a free-for-all nearly always ensued. Mitzi and Spottie would have to retire at a distance and watch the coveted lap jealously.

After a while Koko would see a butterfly, or she would remember a half-eaten banana or a place where she had hidden some peanuts. Then she would hop off to attend to some of her baboon business. When she returned, Spottie and Mitzi would occupy the spot she had so lately occupied. Then was the time for Koko to retire in watchful jealousy. She did it with poor grace, for she was an exceedingly poor loser, and she let the whole neighborhood know about her bad luck. She usually ascended a nearby porch pillar, and from that high vantage point she would punctuate the silence with ear-puncturing yaps and cries. Then she would descend frequently to bite Spottie covertly on the flank or give Mitzi's tail a vicious yank. If they got angry and gave chase, she always worked it so that she got the lap before they had realized what had happened. There she sat, in state, with the smuggest look on her face I ever saw.

Koko never saw a snake or a leopard, for she had been reared entirely by us. Yet she must have known something about the danger of these enemies of her kind. She sensed the danger through instinct. One day a length of hose lay in the long grass; it looked for all the world like a snake. Koko hopped over toward it to examine it from a safe distance. I could hear her disapproving yap-yaps from the house as she scolded that length of hose. Then I went out onto the porch; and she ran to me, ascended me as if I were a tree, and chittered and emitted long-drawn "ah-h-h-hs" for several minutes.

On another day Daddy Lee got my big leopard skin rug, tied it around his waist, and came out on the porch where Koko sat on my lap. Although she could see only the skin rippling over Daddy Lee's knees, danger spoke to her heart. With one anguished "ah-h-h-h," she left my lap like a flash and climbed to the top of the highest tree, and she did not descend until nightfall.

As she got older, we made her stay in an immense cage we built for her. It was as big as a small room and was equipped with swings and all sorts of bars. But it was not freedom, and Koko loved freedom very much. But she had got into so much mischief in the house, and had broken so many eggs and dishes, and knocked over lamps that she had to be banished. But I went into her cage and played with her every day. She spent hours working with the fasteners on her cage, and she frequently got out. Always, however, she came directly to the house. I awoke from an afternoon nap several times to find the cuddly little creature snuggled up to me, fast asleep. Poor little Koko! Her love of freedom proved to be her undoing. Often she stealthily undid the fasteners of her cage and came and spent the night on top of one of the pillars on the veranda. That was never a safe place, for wild beasts often roam the mission at nighttime, attracted by chickens or pets. A leopard raked her down one night as she sat on her high perch sleeping. I will never forget her, for she was a sweet little pet. I suppose when she felt the ugly claws of the leopard, she must have called me to come and help her. She must have cried out, "Ah-h-h-h," very loudly, but I did not hear her. And the next day seemed empty without little Koko.

Daina's Strange Vacation

SCHOOL was out at the mission station; and Daina, together with several other mission students of the girl's school, had walked all the long way home. Twenty-two miles might seem like a long way to old people with stiff joints or to people who are old and sick. But to four bright girls in their teens, girls who were healthy and happy, it seemed as nothing. The miles just flew out from under their willing feet. They had started out toward their village near the old Tekerani Mission some twenty odd miles from Malamulo while the dew was still trembling on the long, tangled grasses.

Every girl had her *katundu,* or load, made up of her blanket, books, clothes, and other small possessions tied up tightly so she could carry it on her head. Each girl had a lunch, too. Mangoes were ripe, and the girls knew of several big trees where the rich fruit hung ripe and yellow in ravines and bypaths near the main road. They might even find a large golden-ripe papaya, which gives as much strength in the eating as a meal of rice and sweet potatoes.

So, chattering gaily, the girls sped along their way. The road they followed went through the huge Makwasa Tea Estate. The fields and the hills and the valleys were full of the lovely terraced rows of tea bushes. But they had to be careful, for the rows were full of heathen young men picking tea, who called out saucy remarks to the girls; but Daina and her friends hurried right on by without a look or an answer. The teachers at the mission had constantly, yes, daily warned the students against intermarriage with the heathen. Every night the drums of the Makwasa beer dances could be heard amid the screams and yells of the drunken dancers.

No, neither Daina nor her friends wanted to find husbands among such as these. The men knew how to make little reed traps to catch rats and mice, which were considered rare delicacies. They ate other things: certain kinds of worms and beetles, monkeys, baboons, and the ugly long-tusked wild hog. The girls well knew from observation what their lives would be like if they were linked with the heathen.

The road to Tekerani is beautiful. Great trees, towering hills, and deep valleys made the simple road, narrow as it is, extremely hard to build. However, in fine weather motor cars can go on it if drivers watch out for sharp curves and washouts. On bad days the road often gets impassable.

When Daina and her friends reached the home village, the whole populace was expecting them. So few things happen in their simple lives that even the homecoming of some girls is regarded as an event. The mothers and fathers had prepared a feast, a Christian feast, and had invited several friends to hear what their children had to say about their life in the mission. They never tired of hearing of the doings of the white people. Some of the things they did amused them until they laughed and laughed. When the girls told them that some of the white women have gardens just for flowers, they were as amazed as they were amused.

"Why, do those white ones eat the *maluwa?*" they asked. It was beyond their understanding that one should use good seeds, and good ground, and good time, and good water for something he could not eat or wear on his body.

The Daina laughed. "No, they do not eat the *maluwa,* but they told me that it is good to be seeing pretty things. They said the eyes need food just as the stomach does. They said that if we do not like the pretty things, why do we get the red and the orange cloth? Why don't we get black all the time?"

The old ones pondered this. Why, there was something true in it. A red cloth made the heart feel happier than an ugly goatskin. They would have to think about it for a while.

For the feast the old ones had roasted fat sweet potatoes in the coals. A certain mealie bread had been made and baked in an oven dug into the ground. There were pots of fluffy valley rice, hot and good, to be eaten with a salty relish, or *ndiwo* made of tomatoes, onions, and cabbage.

After the food was eaten, there were long stalks of sugar cane to chew on and enjoy. Next they had pulled out the mats so they could sit around the fire. Then Daina resumed her story of her life at the mission school. Hardly one of her hearers could read or write, and many of them had come out of raw heathenism. They were naturally curious about a life they were too old ever to share.

So she told them of the school, of the classes, and of chapel, where all the students met to worship the great God. She told of the church services and the songs the people had learned to sing.

"And we girls have a place for going to school and for learning. There is a building which has a long room, and in this room are machines for sewing."

Nearly everyone knew about the machine for sewing, for the Singer machine is in nearly every village in central Africa. Nearly every African woman has two or three humble ambitions, and a big one or two. The humble ones are for teapots, cups, saucers, and plates, blankets, and sheet beds. The big ones are for a sewing machine and a gramophone, as they call a record player. But not all of them understand just how the sewing machine works, and if they had one, they would not know what to do with it. Daina explained to the old ones how the machine worked.

"All you do," she said, "is to turn a wheel at one end with your hand—though some of the machines run like a potter's wheel by the feet. Then a sharp needle begins to pick into the cloth, sewing it together. But you have to be careful while you are allowing the cloth to go in under the needle. It goes so fast that the needle can easily sew the finger or the thumb. Once I sewed my finger and had to go to the doctor to have him fix it."

"*Nzodabwitsa*," said her old father, for he thought it was nothing short of wonderful that just iron and wheels which had no life could be taught to do such marvelous things. He took the cloth into his hands and examined it very closely.

Then Daina brought out her knitting. She carried it in a strong bag she had made to carry her sewing materials in. She had knitted a pair of red socks for her father. He was overjoyed with the gift, even though he had never owned a pair of shoes. Now an unquenchable ambition sprang up in the old man's heart. To own and wear a pair of shoes would make him one of the most important men in all the village—especially if he wore with them the bright socks which his own girl had made for him.

"I will save these until I am able to buy myself some

shoes," he cried out, his old voice quivering with pride. Already he was planning how he would wrap these beautiful things in a cloth and show them to all the men and women in every village around. Then they would see for themselves what wonderful things an educated girl can do. This would stop the mouths of some who criticized him for allowing his girl to go to school and get learning. They were always saying that a heathen wife is much less troublesome to a man than a Christian wife. Only yesterday one had said to him:

"If a man has a heathen wife, she will not trouble her husband to be buying this thing and that thing at the Indian stores; and when a man gets a few shillings, he can spend it on a few bracelets for himself, or some cloth for a shirt, or a few cigarettes, such as are sent in from other lands. Educated girls are always troubling their husbands to buy cups and plates and blankets and cloth with flowers on it. They even refuse to eat with their fingers, as we have always done, and want the men to buy spoons, which are foolishness."

Daina's father carefully put the beautiful socks away where the ants, the rats, and the cockroaches could not chew on them and spoil them. The next day Daina, with one of her younger sisters, set out for a distant village to visit her mother's people. It happened that her old grandmother lived in the same village as the paramount chief of that area. Kuyesa, the proud chieftain, had many wives, children, dogs, and guns. It was interesting to be in this chief's village, for everyone loved his principal wife. She was friendly with the village people and went around to visit and talk to the people more than any other chieftain's wife, and that made her very popular.

"See? She is not a proud one," they would say. And they

often went to her to tell her their grievances. And if she saw that the complaint was just and good, she took it upon herself to tell the chief all about it. Often she got something done about what was wrong. But woe be to anyone who told her a lie and got her to plead for something that was not good. Then that person lost a friend and did not need ever to come to her again with any kind of grievance or complaint. She would not even listen.

The first morning after Daina got to the home of her grandmother, she was pounding native meal in the big wooden mortar, when along came the chief's principal wife to see the visitor from a distant village.

Of course Daina left off her pounding and ran for her grandmother so she too could enjoy the visit with the chief's principal wife. Then she went into the house and brought out the best mat so they could sit down and chat.

After a while she ran into the kitchen house to revive the coals and put on a pot of water. There was a kind of tea that her grandmother made. Then she found the sugar and was happy that she had brought some little mealie muffins she had made the evening before she came to the village of her grandmother. Luckily her grandmother had three cups which were not broken or cracked. In a little while she was back with three cups of bush tea and a muffin apiece on a wide tin plate. The chief's wife was delighted and kept exclaiming again and again about how good the muffins were. And she had to be told just exactly how they were made, for she wanted to make some for herself. She was a woman just under middle age. Her skin was smooth and a light brown, and her hair had been combed vigorously with the native comb and smoothed back as flat as she could make it. But her eyes were so sad that one looked at them again and again. She had had seven little children, and all but two of them had died of some native disease—beilharzia, malaria, or dysentery. Now she was in constant fear day and night lest the children left to her would die also.

As she sat there talking to Daina, she too asked about the kind of life she had at the mission school. Then she asked whether it was true that the white doctors would kill the people to make medicine out of them, as she had so often heard. Daina hastened to explain that this was not true at all, but was a tale that the witch doctors told because they saw that the hospitals were ruining their bad doings.

"I was going to take my last little girl to the hospital before she died, but so many people told me so many things I was afraid to do so. She died anyway, . . . and she was such a pretty baby. Sometimes in the night I wake up, thinking I hear her soft little voice calling, 'Amai.' Oh, dear, death is a bad thing in this world."

"I know those things are lies, because I worked in the house of the doctor," said Daina. "He is, oh, so kind and good. I knitted some things for their children, and they were always giving me rice and bread and even butter on the bread. Once I stayed all night there to help with the children while one of them had measles. I heard them call for the doctor in the night to come to the hospital. I heard them say that one woman was getting worse. It was raining hard, but the doctor went out in the cold and the rain. I heard his wife ask him when he came home how the poor woman was, and he said, 'She will live. It was a hard fight, but we saved her.' Does that sound like they are bad people?"

"Oh, I wish I had taken little Bethya. Perhaps even now she would be alive to gladden my heart. But, Daina," the chieftain's wife interrupted herself to say, "you say you can knit?"

"Yes, I learned such things as that at the mission school," answered Daina modestly.

"And are you able also to sew on the machine that is made for sewing the clothes for people to wear? Can you make trousers and shirts?" she persisted eagerly.

"Yes, I can do that, too, and I have even cut off patterns from papers for shirts, trousers, and dresses. When we use these patterns, we can make a dress or a shirt and use less cloth than the native tailors do. They cut from guessing and often spoil much cloth for poor people."

"Yes, I know that is so," admitted the chief's wife. "I took some very pretty cloth, blue with bright red flowers, for a little dress for Bethya last year. When the tailor had it made, it was so small she could not get into it. I think he steals cloth to make small baby dresses to sell."

"Yes, there was a *mlandu* [a case to be decided by the headman or chief] near our school," said Daina. "One of the girls got some cloth and said she did not have the time to make herself a dress. She got plenty of cloth, so that she expected to have a full skirt. But when she went to get it from the tailor, the skirt was narrow, the sleeves were tight, and the waist was so small she could hardly fasten it. She is an active girl, and she ran right to the chest and opened it before he could say a word. She found more than a yard and a half of her cloth hidden there. So she went and told the chief."

"I hope the chief made a good decision for her and punished the tailor. But listen, my girl. I have a machine for sewing, and I do not know how to use it. I have knitting needles and two whole buckets of fine wool from England, and I do not know how to knit either."

"I will teach you the little I know," murmured Daina modestly.

Nothing would do, but that Daina must go to the house of the chief right away. She was filled with wonder that this thing should happen to her, and she made up her mind to comfort the good woman if she had a chance, and tell her of the promises in the Bible about the resurrection. If the poor woman knew she could see her little girl some glad day, how happy that would make her!

Daina was used to a typical native house: a house made of mud plastered over a frame of bamboo. There was a porch all around the house so the heavy tropical rains would not wash the little mud house away. But this house, to Daina's untutored eyes, was very grand. It was built of burned bricks and was whitewashed inside. There were ceilings made of matting, there were doors made out of wood, and there was glass in the windows. The wife had hung up some cloth at the windows in an attempt at curtains, but since she did not know how to sew, the results were not pretty. Daina determined to help her with her house as best she could.

Then there was a little furniture. In the middle of the room a long table was covered with a bright oilcloth. There were chairs made by native craftsmen; a narrow homemade cot, covered with a blanket, was at one side. Skins of goats and leopards lay on the mud floor. Poor as it was, it looked grand to Daina, who had always slept on the floor.

The chief's wife darted into one of the side rooms and came out with a hand sewing machine. Daina set it up on the table and opened it. A boy was sent scuttling to the Indian store for thread, and the cloth was gotten out of a large covered box. There were many pieces. They looked over the patterns Daina had brought with her, and it was decided to make a dress for the ten-year-old daughter, who came in to be measured.

All that day Daina showed the woman how to cut, measure, and sew. The basting was hard, for the poor woman hardly knew which hand to hold the needle in. But she was quick to learn and overjoyed at everything that was done. The little dress was done by nightfall, and the child wore it and spilled food all over it as she ate her supper.

Daina had a lot to tell her family that night.

"She was not even able to hold a needle at first," she said, and they all laughed loud and long at such a funny thing. Most of those who laughed the loudest would not have even known which end of the needle to sew with if they had been asked.

Then came the day, after several dresses had been made, that the chief's wife wanted to make a shirt. She had to call the chief in, and Daina showed her how to measure so that the pattern could be adjusted to his size.

Oh dear, thought Daina. A shirt is such a troublesome thing to make. It would be terrible to make it badly or to spoil a piece of good cloth. There were seams, and gussets, and buttonholes, and the neckband, and the collar, and the cuffs. These all were very particular and had to be cut just right or the shirt did not fit well.

After the pattern was laid out on the bright green cloth and pinned ready for the cutting, Daina shut her eyes and offered a little prayer to God for wisdom. She had been taught at the mission school that the Lord is glad to help people even with small things if they ask Him for His help.

"Dear Lord, help me," she whispered. The Lord did help Daina. By the end of the next day the chief had a new shirt which fitted him exactly. She prayed too about the heel of a sock. When she taught the chief's wife to knit, she almost forgot how to turn the heel—till she prayed.

When Daina and her sister decided to go back to her

Daina shut her eyes and offered
a little prayer to God for wisdom.

home village, she had taught the wife of the chief many things. When she went away, the woman gave her cloth for two dresses, and the chief gave her money for her school fees.

But the best thing of all was that the whole village learned that a wise, clever girl is important, even in the household of a chief. And many fathers and mothers decided then and there to send their girls to the mission school so they could be clever like Daina.

Eggs and Twins

IT WAS hard to get good eggs out in the mission field of central Africa. Sometimes I bought eggs from the heathen people who came to the back door of my house to sell things. But they were almost as small as bantam eggs and were so strong they did not taste good to eat by themselves. However, we did use them in cooking. We always had to try them in a pan of water, or we would have gotten rotten eggs more often than not.

After a while I found out that there was a tea planter near the village of Limbe whose wife raised Rhode Island Red hens and roosters. I decided to go see her and ask whether she would sell me a setting of eggs and a couple of hens and a rooster. We could not go into town too often, because gasoline is high-priced and hard to get sometimes. But as soon as I could, I went in to see Mrs. Tucker. She was gracious to me, and in a little while we went out to the elaborate enclosure where she kept her chickens.

The hens just walked right up to her and ate corn out of her hand while she was talking to them as if they were small children. She petted them and talked to them. I could see she had made pets out of them. She picked up two fluffy, amiable-looking hens and talked to them and even

102

explained why she was selling them. She assured each old hen that here was another mamma who would love her just as much as she did. One hen she called Sarah, and the other was named Betsey. I fancied that Sarah looked at me a little critically. I hoped she and Betsey would approve of me and do the best they could in the matter of laying eggs.

Even though Mrs. Tucker was loud in her praise of the two hens, I could not help but notice we had no testimony meeting about the rooster. She had sent a native boy to get him, and he was in the box when we arrived to incarcerate the hens. I found out why I did not have any statement of his merits. I found it out to my sorrow, for that red rooster was as dangerous as a stick of dynamite. He attacked everyone, on no provocation whatsoever. As soon as I let him out of the box in the hen yard, he made for me and slashed my legs in several places before I could make any defense. Then he backed up to come at me again. Since there was no escape and because he was coming fast, I kicked at him just as he closed in. As luck would have it, I laid him out cold. I thought, Oh dear, here I have paid twenty-five shillings for a fine rooster, and I've killed him before I had him an hour. But after a few minutes he got up and went on the other side of the hen house to regain his composure. Betsey had gone to hunt a nest and was even then turning round and round getting it fixed to suit her fancy. Sarah was singing to beat the band. I had half a dozen small native hens who laid sporadically and were always wanting to set. I put the setting of eggs under one of them.

The rooster's bad temper continued, so I named him Mussolini H. Stalin and called him Hitler for short. I learned that I did not dare to enter the hen yard for eggs or even to bring feed and water without a stick or a stout piece

I did not dare to enter the hen yard for eggs or
even to bring feed and water without a stick.

of bamboo. I had to keep my eye on the old rascal, though,
for he had a way of sneaking up behind me, and his spurs
were sharp.

There was a wildcat that used to come and catch small
chicks of other missionaries. As soon as this cat found out
that I had chickens, he paid a visit to our hen house. He
did not come the second time. Hitler flew at him with such
a blitzkrieg that the fierce old cat almost regretted the day
he was born. I got so I appreciated my fierce old rooster a
little after that. When I let the chickens out to forage for
themselves in the late afternoon, no cat, or dog, or even
native child dared to come close to where he was watching
over his little harem. There would be real trouble if they
did.

Sarah and Betsey were fine hens and got right down to the job of laying without any monkey business at all. After a few days I discovered a curious fact about Sarah. Every day or so, she laid a very queer-looking, elongated egg. It was almost as long again as an ordinary egg, and much bigger around. Around the middle of the egg was a raised egg shell ridge, as if old Sarah had decided to lay two eggs at once and then glue them together in the middle. About that time one of the nervous, erratic native hens wanted to set. I wanted to put big eggs under her, but oh dear. Seven of those big eggs I had had the cook boy save for setting were those monster eggs of Sarah's.

People always told me if I would set a double-yolked egg, the chickens would be fastened together like Siamese twins. But these eggs were so very big, I decided to try anyway. I put only the big eggs under the tiny little hen. She had a lapful at that and clucked angrily as she wiggled and tried to adjust herself on the biggest eggs she had ever dreamed of sitting on in her short life. I tried to keep my experiment to myself, for I did not want everybody shouting at me and saying, "I told you so," if everything went wrong. But murder will out. The native help found out about it first and then my husband, and all were telling me that I had wasted seven eggs that would have been wonderful scrambled or creamed. But I waited. I had the date that the setting would hatch all marked on the calendar, and I eagerly awaited the day. They were to hatch on a Sunday morning.

I went out to the hen house at daybreak. Something *was* happening under that little native hen's apron. She looked angry, upset, and short-tempered, and scolded me in several native dialects. I was so anxious to find out what was up that I picked her up in spite of her squawks.

There was one empty shell and *two,* yes, TWO fluffy, yellow chicks. Every one of the other big eggs was pipped. I waited (even helping a little) and oh joy! Yes! Two more! By nightfall I was the proud possessor of fourteen Rhode Island Red chicks, very little smaller than if they had each had an egg to develop in. I do not know which one was the prouder: I or my native hen.

I could give voice to my satisfaction, and I *could* tell everyone, even doubting Thomases, that I had an old hen which laid twin eggs.

Tsoka

LONG ago, at the beginning of the century, Mala-mulo Mission was just a small clearing in the dense forests of central Africa. There were no doctors or nurses there at the time, just a good, kind mission director and his small staff of native teachers.

Everything was primitive, and no one dreamed of having a car. There were no electric lights any place around, much less on an isolated mission station far out in the bush country. The town nearest to Malamulo was Blantyre, forty miles across the bush, and the only way to get there was to follow the grassy paths. Nobody went very far from home unless the business was urgent.

When the director's wife needed salt or sugar or matches or a piece of cloth, she had to send native carriers to go and get the things for her. Mail did not come often, and it took many weeks for a letter to travel from Africa to America or England.

If the missionaries needed to go to town, they rode in queer hammocklike devices. These were swung from poles and carried by strong natives. They ran on a swift dogtrot, and the rough, swaying hammock was tiresome before the long journey was completed. You may be sure they did not go on trips very often in those days. You could not be sure you would not meet a lion or a leopard on the road either. You just had to hope for the best.

Even though there was no doctor at the mission in those days, many, many sick people came to the mission for help. It was a little frightening to do anything for these poor people, because they were usually very sick indeed and came to the white man only as a last resort. It was not unusual for the person to be dead when the people would arrive, or very near to death. Then the mission director had to tell the people that they had come too late. He could do nothing when they had waited so long. It was all very sad.

It was true that when they got home, even if the white doctor did not do a thing, the witch doctor always told the people, "You see, I told you it would be so. The white man has killed this man. He had a medicine in his eyes that he can kill by just looking at a person or touching with the hands. Why, if he touches the head the smallest bit, you can have a headache so that it feels as if your head will fall off your neck."

"But," the people often argued, "he was almost dead anyway, and he was not killed."

"It is too bad that you do not believe my words," the witch doctor would retort angrily. "But I will tell you one thing: I am glad you brought back his body so that we may have the funeral here and see him buried in the ground. The white man often kills the black people to make his medicine and to eat him. That is a fact."

Even though the people hated and feared the witch doctor, he scared them so much that they used his charms until they saw he was not helping them a bit. Then they tried to sneak the sick one away when the witch doctor went to the garden or to another village. And sometimes, indeed, many times, the person got well. When this happened, the witch doctor had little to say. Or he would laugh and say that the person was not even sick, so no wonder he got well.

But one day the village people brought Tsoka, a poor little boy about ten years of age, to the mission. It was plain to see that he was near death. His eyes looked enormous in his little thin face, and his cheeks were sunken until he looked like a wrinkled old man. His little body was nothing but skin stretched over bones, with ugly festering scabs all over him. He looked as though he had never had a bath in all his life. But that was not true. Africans bathe very often, if they are near enough to water to do so.

The native carriers set the machila down in front of the mission school and went in to fetch the *bwana*. He came out, wondering what miserable plight this poor human being was in, and what he could do for him.

The big raw-boned native who helped carry the little fellow was the spokesman. He tried to tell the *bwana* that they had done all they could, but this great sore on Tsoka's back kept getting bigger and bigger. Then he turned the child over so the *bwana* could see his back.

Accustomed as he was to horrible things, to gaping wounds, to raging fevers, the good man still gasped at what he saw. He had never seen anything like it in all his life. It was a terrible ulcer all over the whole back, red, raw, and angry—the biggest ulcer he had ever seen. He gasped in horror when the carrier lifted the wilted banana leaves with which they had covered it. The little boy looked into the white man's face piteously. It was as if he were saying, "What more will I have to suffer? Will you be able to make me well, or will you, too, fail as all the rest have done?" The kind eyes of the man lingered on the little face. The two looked at each other, one measuring the other, both questioning. The little one might have said, "Must I die? Do I have to die? I am so little and young, and my life is barely begun."

Then the native teacher, who had followed the *bwana* out from the school building, whispered, "Oh, I would say, sir, by all means, do not take him. Do not consider it for even a moment. He is sure to die, and you know how they always are blaming us for death, even if the person is dead when he gets here!"

But the mission director must have felt intuitively that here lay a giant among men, even though he was sick unto death. He turned to the teacher. "Ever hear of the doctor who was called on a winter night to attend a miner's child in Wales? His folks urged him not to go and said, 'What's one less child among the miners anyway?' Well, the babe he saved that night was David Lloyd George, so the story goes. And who am I to say that this lad, if my poor efforts will save him, may not be a mighty man in the work of the Lord someday?" Then he directed the carriers to take the child to the clinic. He would be there as soon as he could get some things together.

As he and the teacher were on their way to the clinic, the director said again, "I could not send that child away. Did you see how he looked up at me so pitifully? I can hardly know how he feels, for I have never faced almost certain death as he is doing. I will do all I can and leave the rest up to God. All things are possible with Him, you know."

It was not long until five boys came carrying water, soap, and clean cloths. Someone made up one of the crude cots with clean sheets and a dark blanket. A table was brought near, and Tsoka was lifted tenderly and laid face down on the table. Then the hard part began, for the wound was frightfully dirty. The child tried not to cry, but the pain was so fearful he could not help it.

After the wound was cleansed and dressed, the slashing pains were not so bad. Then Tsoka was bathed all over and slipped into a clean shirtlike garment. He was given a dish of rice and some ripe bananas. He fell asleep then and slept for several hours.

He was given good food, well-cooked, and at regular times. He got beans, peas, pumpkin, rice, cabbage, tomatoes, and onions. Not once did they bring him cooked rat or mouse, and these people did not seem to favor black fish either.

His body was regularly bathed, and the ulcer was dressed every day. The medicine hurt so much that Tsoka cried pitifully every time he saw the dressers coming with the dressings. But it hurt a little less every day, though he did not realize it at the time.

As usual after his wound was dressed, he was bathed and given some good food to eat. He always went to sleep then and slept for a long time. Gradually he was getting well, but it was so gradual that many weeks went by before he himself realized it. The mission director saw the improvement and was glad and thanked God. The dressers saw it and marveled. People were praying for little Tsoka, though he did not learn about that until afterward.

One bright morning he awoke early. As he lay there, he noticed that he had turned over and was lying on his *back*. His back! He lay there hardly able to believe this wonderful thing. Then he knew he was getting well. He was so happy that he began to laugh and laugh and laugh softly. He did not want to make much noise, for an old man who was very sick with malaria and pneumonia was lying in the cot beside his.

Now, he thought, I do not have to die. I do not have to die. The child had seen death many times, and he had dreaded most of all the time when the people would wrap him up and put him into a deep hole in the ground. It did not seem possible that he would know nothing about it.

He stretched his arms cautiously. No! The pains were only small complaining hurts, not the slashing agonies he had gotten used to. Now he could stretch with only a little pain. He laughed again.

Then he saw the native man coming with the dressing basket and the medicines to dress his wound. He looked up impishly when he was turned over on his stomach, and even though it did hurt, he did not cry this time. Why, even yesterday he had cried a little, just because he had gotten in the habit of it, for his wound was hurting less and less all the time.

"You are a good boy," the native nurse said when he was through. "And you are going to get well now. Even I did not think there was any hope for you. I begged the *bwana* to send you away."

"But he did not send me," stated Tsoka gleefully, laughing softly. "And I did not die as you all thought I would. I thought I would myself."

"Do you know why you did not die, my child?" The native nurse stopped and looked the child full in the face. Tsoka looked up at him wonderingly.

"Why, yes, I know," he answered childishly. "The witchcraft of the white man and his strong medicine. They know the ways of chasing away the evil spirits that cause sickness."

"My boy," the native teacher said solemnly, "you got well because of the God of the white people, the God they came to our country to tell us about. I think you have heard about the great *Bwana* Livingstone, who chased slavery out of this country. All Africans have heard about him, for our land has peace now. This God is the same one as *Bwana* Livingstone came to tell the African people to serve. He is a strong God, and He has made everything you see and everything there is on this whole world."

"Did the white ones bring Him to Africa?" asked Tsoka curiously.

"No one can take or bring this God," answered the teacher. "He lives on high, up above the clouds and above everything, and He can see everything in the world at the same time. This white *bwana* here is one-who-knows-God. I have seen and heard him talk to God; and I, Dzenje, I also talk to God. He is my God also. And I hope you will take Him to be your God, since He has done so much for you."

"What does He look like, Dzenje?" asked Tsoka curiously. "Is He big and tall and very white? Does He wear clothes and have the hairs on his face as this *bwana* has?"

All the time that they were talking, Dzenje was cleaning things up, clearing the table, closing the ointments, wrapping the dirty dressings so they could be washed and used again; but he stopped short and looked at Tsoka sharply.

"Boy," he cried in horror, "no man has seen God. But it was He who made the heavens and the earth, and He made you well."

The native nurse started out, but when he got to the door, he turned around.

"The *bwana* said that you may walk around the mission some today. Do not sit in the hot sun or get too tired. And above all things, do not scratch your wound, no matter how much it itches. A wound getting well always itches."

"You tell me that every day," laughed Tsoka.

"Well, I want you to remember it every day," the teacher retorted. "Why don't you go over to the school and see how

8   113

the boys are learning? You might take it into your head to learn a thing or two yourself."

Tsoka ate his *nsima ndi ndiwo* and the big yellow papaya which Dzenje had brought to him. Then he slipped off his bed cautiously and tried the floor with his legs. He almost fell when he tried to stand, and the room got all dark for a few minutes, just as if he was going to faint. After a while he got up and slowly made his way to the porch, and he sat down and rested awhile. Then little by little, as he had strength, he made his way down the little hill where the school was located.

He slipped in, sat down on the floor in the back, and leaned against the wall. A teacher named Morrison Malinki was up in front teaching the boys something, but Tsoka could not make out for a while what it was all about.

The teacher had a chart up in front. On it were marks like the scratching of hens in the mud. It was puzzling at first, and it seemed that the boys could tell some scratches from other scratches, and called each bunch of scratches by name. It was all curious, until he noticed that there were some marks just like other marks. They had the same name if they looked just exactly alike. But they had to be alike. He heard them say, "Ona," then they said, "Ana." These were almost alike, but not quite. Then he sat up quickly. He was beginning to see. He could tell Ana from Ona. He listened, watched, and was alert every minute. Before that class was over, he knew every word on the chart. The teacher saw his interested face and said loudly, "You, boy back there; you have just come in. Do you think you could tell me at least one word on this chart? Some of these boys have been learning for many days and do not know them yet."

"Let me try, sir," he said modestly.

Malinki, the teacher, took his pointer and started at the top. To everybody's surprise, Tsoka knew every word.

"Oh, but he has been to some other school," said one young man.

"Have you?" asked Malinki.

"I have never even seen a school until this day," replied Tsoka humbly. "I just watched and listened. I learned from what the others said the words were."

All the boys began to work harder when they saw what a sick boy had done in one day. And he liked school so well he never missed another day thereafter.

It has been more than forty years since Tsoka was carried to the mission for healing. He had been only a shadow of a child, with a horrible ulcer sapping his life away. Now Tsoka is an ordained minister and the head of one of the cleanest, most orderly missions in all Nyasaland. Some of his children are in the work of the Lord. Some are in school. But all of them are Christians and are looking for the coming of the Lord. Tsoka has reared his whole family to know God. He would have been dead, buried, and forgotten long ago if it had not been for a godly missionary who saw in him a precious jewel for the kingdom of God.

Amos

FEW AFRICAN babies ever travel as far as did tiny Amos. He had been only three days old when his young mother, Ndamvelekina, and Kasonga, his father, ran away from a life of slavery in the port of Bwani on the Indian Ocean.

Of course he could really remember nothing of the journey, but he had heard his father and mother tell and retell it around the fire at night so often that he felt almost as if he did remember. So Amos often told his small brothers, Philip and Cosalawa, the stories as if he did.

"We had traveled for weeks and weeks and weeks. I think we were almost at the other side of the world. Then when we were going around a mountain, we saw a lion. Oh, I tell you we were scared, and we all ran and climbed trees."

"You did not," cried Cosalawa angrily. "You were too little. Amai had you on her back. She said so. Your eyes weren't even open yet."

"They were too, and people are not like cats and dogs. Their eyes are open when they are born."

But it all seemed real to Amos. Very, very real. And it seemed as if he could remember.

But Amos went to school and learned to read from the chart. He learned to write with a sharp stick on the ground. And he learned to count and to figure a little. Kasonga was proud of his boy. He was not such a small boy, though, when at the mission located at Tsapa. He must have been a tall lad in his late teens, though he had no idea how old he was. It was the usual thing for grown men to attend school in those early days.

The mission director about this time began to teach Amos the work of a blacksmith. In a mud hut back of the schoolhouse he had a forge and an anvil. There he learned to blow the fire with the leather bellows until even iron got red-hot and had to be handled with tongs. He wore an apron made from the skin of a cow to keep the hot sparks from burning his body.

The white people on the mission got an oil from faraway countries called kerosene. This strange substance looked for all the world like water, but it burned as the fat of the goat or the wild pig, only it did not sputter and fry and smell bad while it was burning. With this oil the white ones had lamps which made beautiful bright lights for their houses. They were able to read from books and even to sew clothing with needles and thread in the night as well as in the day.

This oil came in large, bright tins, each of which was measured to contain what the white man said was four English gallons. These empty tins were wonderful for carrying water, for everyone knows that pots break easily and are heavy before one starts to the water hole to get the water. Then when they are full, they are very heavy indeed.

From these empty tins Amos was taught to make many things. He made small round tin pans which were good for cooking food over a fire. He was taught to turn up beadlike seams until the pans were strong and did not leak. He made pails, little troughs for feeding chickens, and cans with a long spout full of holes for watering plants in the gardens.

Amos fixed the harness of the oxen and did general repairing everywhere. He became an important man on the mission. It was too bad old Kasonga had died. He would have been proud of his children, for all three of them went into the work of the Lord.

Many years of fruitful labor went by. Amos was content and happy. He was put in charge of the mill which ground grain for the school. There was custom grinding too. People from the villages round about brought their meal to be ground. They paid in meal for this service. In this way Amos helped to earn the food which the mission students ate. He was a great help to the mission until he got into trouble.

The wife of Amos was not a good woman. She did not have the high principles and a sense of honor that Kasonga had drilled into Amos. Ndamvelekina had not liked her, and when she spoke of her to Kasonga, she had called her Mkazi Yezebeli, because that was a bad woman she had heard lived back in Bible times.

Her name was Aluya. She had quarrels and even fights with the other women of the village. Nobody liked her very well, and Amos was sorry. He was a quiet, peaceful man and would have liked an orderly household.

After he began the business of grinding the grain, she came one day to get her meal ground. She did not have quite enough for a good meal, and she saw it was easy (when Amos was not looking) to fill up the small bag she had. She went home elated. So she made some excuse to go every day on some pretext or the other and got all the meal she needed for each day from the mission supply of meal.

Now she had much more time on her hands, and she could range all over the village and other villages, and she got into more fights and quarrels than you could shake a stick at. She thought she was having a great time.

Amos was slow and unobserving, so he did not notice or suspect what was going on right under his nose. This went on for several months. Planting time came. Amos told Aluya to help him clear the garden for planting when the rains came. But she tossed her saucy head and laughed right in his face.

"Me? I shall not hoe or plant this year. It is not necessary."

Amos's mouth fell open. Had his wife gone mad?

"Are you crazy?"

Then Aluya told Amos what had been going on for many months. She told it boldly, proudly, brazenly, as if she had done a great favor for her husband and was worthy of praise.

But Amos did not praise her. He dropped his head to his arms. Now all the glory and the honor of his work had been stripped away. He learned what it was to walk, live, and eat with fear. His food, stolen as it was, did not taste sweet any more. His wife had done more than take what they were eating; she was now going to the market and selling a little every day and getting money for cloth, and cups, and plates, and spoons. The terrible part was that she was a blabber mouth. He felt that everyone must know by now what was going on. But she stoutly defended herself.

"I have brought many new customers from other villages to the mill. You know that. And I think I should have some of the mealie meal for the trouble I go to in getting people to walk so far."

With her wheedling, her coaxing, and her loose justifying

and even outright threats Amos tried to tell himself that it was nothing, that it was of no importance. But then he was further terrified to notice that the wife of Tenford, his helper, began to come often, yes, several times in a day to the mill. He saw that she came with an empty bag, and when she went away, it was bulging. He saw her hands in the meal, stealing boldly, with defiant eyes right on his face; but he dared not say a word. Aluya, his wife, was at it too.

Tenford and Amos did not know, but eyes saw
every handful of meal the evil women took.

Then Amos stopped praying in the morning and at night, for the joy and the brightness had gone out of his life. He grew afraid of his shadow. If he saw the *bwana* mission director coming up the road to meet him, he was more than likely to go off into the bush to avoid him. His life became a burden to him. He became afraid of Cosalawa, too. He was a man of honor. He had a good wife, who attended to her own affairs and was seldom seen about the mission. Everyone trusted Cosalawa even as he had been honored and trusted through the years. Cosalawa carried the keys to all the food storage bins of the whole school.

One night Amos almost hit his wife. He was sorry for that, for he knew that true Christians do not hit one another. True Christian white men never beat native people. True husbands never beat their wives. While he was eating his porridge on that particular night, Aluya came in and sat down on the mat near to him.

"I have been thinking, Amos," she said.

He grunted, not encouraging her, for it seemed to him sometimes that he almost hated her. This was not good either, for the Bible plainly says, "Husbands, love your wives" as your own bodies.

"Amos, I have learned where Cosalawa hides the keys to the *bwana's* storehouse when he goes to sleep at night. We can easily get them, and he will never know they have been gone, for we can return them the same night. You know very well that the mission watchman is a lazy fellow and crawls up on the bags of maize and sleeps all night."

Amos had stopped his eating and had turned to look at his wife. The fire flickered so brightly that he could fairly see the glint of evil in her eyes.

"Well," he said ominously.

"Tonight is the dark of the moon and here is our chance. Let us take an empty bag, each of us. We can get rice, cassava, bananas, and beans. He will not notice if we get a little. It will be easier than hoeing, sowing, and planting."

But Amos had leaped to his feet. "Woman," he shouted thickly, "I should beat you as a man beats a dog. You have sent me crazy now, until I run from my shadow. Now I will tell you one thing, and do not forget it. If you touch, yes, I say even touch the keys of Cosalawa, I will go to the white *bwana* myself and tell him to send us both to the jail. Jail is better than fear!"

But the white *bwana* had noted the attitude of Amos the faithful, Amos the good. He had seen how he avoided him. He was a student of human nature enough that he knew by such actions that Amos was carrying a miserable load on his heart. Then quietly he began to investigate. Tenford did not know, Amos did not know, but eyes saw every handful of meal the evil women took. Faithful men who hated to see the work of the Lord in disrepute walked miles and verified the fact that the meal of the Lord was sold in the native markets. Faithful men reported the whole thing.

At last the day came when the evidence was conclusive and so plain that to deny would be foolishness. Tenford and Amos were called to the director's office. Both of them agreed nervously that they would have to lie. They would have to deny everything. There was nothing else to do. Amos was in worse slavery than ever Kasonga had been in faraway Bwani. It is the truth that makes people free.

The evidence, true and irrefutable, was presented, oh, so kindly. Amos looked at the *bwana's* face in misery. He had been so kind, oh, so kind. He wished he could fall to his knees and confess everything: the horrors of the past year, the sorrow, and the unhappiness. But Tenford sat there, angry and loudly denying things that even a baby could see were all true. And because his guilt was tied up with the guilt of the younger man, he had to sit there and deny and deny and deny. The *bwana* prayed and talked quietly. Amos almost wished he would shout and treat him roughly and rudely as he had seen worldly men treat their servants and workers. Even when he asked them to kneel and pray with him, he could not pray.

When they arose, the *bwana* said kindly, "Then, since you both refuse to admit things that everyone, even the heathen, knows are true, you will have to go. We must have people who have a sense of honor for the things which belong to the Lord. Let me have your keys."

For the first time in thirty years Amos sat at home idle. And the year ahead was terrible. They had not sowed or planted. How, then, could they reap? The wives had diligently sold all the meal they stole above their daily needs, so they knew real hunger. They could not eat the teacups or the bright pieces of cloth the stolen meal had bought.

During that long year Amos knew that he was a lost man. He did not go to church. He left off praying. He was in an agony lest he die, or perhaps even the Lord might come and he could never live in the earth made new. Finally he could bear it no longer. He would arise and go, even as the prodigal did in the Bible. Of course he could never hope to get his old job again, but he would be free of the crushing load of sin.

The *bwana* was kind and did not blame him in any way. He listened sympathetically as, weeping and trembling, the unhappy black man told the whole story. Then he told how he had planned to restore what his wife had taken even if it took him to the end of his days.

After he and the *bwana* had prayed, Amos arose from his knees and smiled, yes, actually smiled. It had been so long since he had felt like smiling.

"Ah, *bwana,* the load has fallen from my shoulders. I am so happy, so happy."

"Yes, yes," replied the *bwana* happily. "It is true, Amos, that the 'truth shall make you free.' "

"Yes, *bwana*."

"I believe in you. I have always believed in you. I do not think this was your doing at all, only as you were caught in a trap not of your making. I believe you are truly repentant. Can you come back to your old job? We have never had anyone who could do as well as you did."

"O *bwana*," choked Amos. It seemed as if there could be no joy on earth equal to the joy of being by his forge in the mill room again.

"And I believe you need us as badly as we need you. Do you think you can rule your household so that your wife will not rule over you again?"

Amos began to weep.

"Oh, in this year, *bwana*, we have both tasted of the bitterness. She knows and she, too, has repented. The women of the village have all despised her for dragging her family in the mud, for bringing us all to shame. Our children have suffered, and there has been the hunger, never enough food. It was a bitter medicine we made for our own stomachs."

"Then come back to the old work, Amos, the forge, and, yes, the mill. I trust you, and may the Lord bless you."

So old Amos, wiser and better, old Amos, who knows now what real slavery is, has escaped from his place of slavery and is now the blacksmith on the mission station.

Roy John, Son of Tsoka

A T A LONELY mission station many miles from any town or trading post is a native African teacher named Roy John Tsoka. Long years before, his father had a terrible ulcer on his back, but he was healed by prayer and loving care. It was at that time that he learned to know and to love the gentle Jesus.

Roy John is something like his father. He is quiet, good, and dependable. He has a quiet, neat wife who knows how to sew and knit, and she keeps a clean, orderly home for Roy John and their two little children.

Even though they are poor, their house is as nice as young Mrs. Tsoka knows how to make it. Of course she cannot ever scrub her floor, because it is made out of mud. But every once in a while she muds it again. It gets dusty and rough, and then she knows very well it is time to do something about it. She gets a pot and goes down to the stream and tries to find the blackest, smoothest mud there is along the bank. She makes it like thick porridge and smooths it all over her floor. Then she makes the children stay outside until it gets dry and hard. She thinks it looks nice when she is through.

Her house is made of mud, plastered onto a framework

of bamboo. Roy John has made a kind of water paint out of an almost white clay, and he has painted his house inside and out.

Most heathen people sleep on mats on the floor, but Roy John took a certain soft kind of wood and made beds for his whole family. He feels that it is more civilized to sleep on beds than on the floor. He has little money, so he is careful to raise almost all his food and to make as many of his necessities as he can, so that the money can be used for clothing. Every year he and his wife make a large garden. If they have too much, young Mrs. Tsoka takes some to the market to sell, so they can have a little extra money. She is a good, thrifty wife, and Roy John is justly proud of her.

The rains usually come about the middle of November. Then everyone—men, women, little children, and even old grandfathers and grandmothers—goes out to the mealie lands to plant. They know that if they do not take advantage of the rains and plant while the ground is right, there may be great hunger in the villages. They plant cassava, which is a long, ugly brown root and tastes something like potato when it is baked in hot ashes. We eat it in America, but we call it tapioca. They plant corn, lots of it, for that is their main food. It is both bread and cereal for them. There must be a big sweet potato field, for everyone likes to eat them, boiled or baked in hot ashes. Then there are sugar cane, kaffir corn, eggplant, onions, and cabbage. They also have a queer vine, with a fruit that tastes something like a cucumber, but it has thorns on it. It is called *pwepwete*. If there is a good harvest in the garden, the family eats well. If there is a poor one, hunger and disease walk in the villages.

In 1949 Roy John and his wife, with all the others,

cleared their gardens to get ready for the rains. The hoeing was all done; all the ridging was done. They had their seeds in readiness; just as soon as it would rain, they would plant. November came. Everybody was gay and full of hope. The old corn was weevily and tasted musty, and the promise of fresh, good food was sweet. But the rains did not come. November passed—the whole month. This was strange. Did it not rain always on the eleventh or twelfth every year? The people could talk of nothing else. Why didn't the rains come? What had happened in the sky?

Then the old people began to recall times in the long ago when the rains were late in coming. They told of famines when men, women, and little children all over the land died. Roy John's heart was filled with fear. What would become of his wife and his little ones if this was to be a famine year?

Surely it would rain soon in December, but December came and went, and the sky was like molten brass. The sun boiled down upon the earth in the hottest December the people had known. The little biting insects made life a misery. Wild beasts, hungry and thirsty, came right into the villages. The water holes and the streams dried up, and when one went to hunt for water for drinking, he saw the tracks of wild beasts in the oozing, stinking mud.

January came. No rain. The situation was growing desperate. People were openly afraid. A man who had several bags of grain stored away sat up at night to watch them. Thieves came that night and killed him and took all his grain. Then the pastor of the mission church called the people together and appointed a day of fasting and prayer, that the heaven might open, and the blessed rain might come to refresh the earth.

This was a solemn time. The heathen heard about the

meeting, and they wondered. Evil times of strife and blood-shed were ahead unless the Lord saw fit to answer their prayers. People everywhere were hungry.

Roy John and his wife prayed most earnestly, and it was not much trouble to fast; they had little food to eat. Every day the little wife went far into the bush hunting for foods to eat. One day the sun had been bright and hot when they went for prayer. But on the way home Roy noticed that the sky seemed to be darkening a little bit. By noon the whole sky was filled with clouds, and the lightning was terrific. The thunder kept up a constant bombardment, as if it wanted to make up for all the time it had lost. But it was as the sweetest music to the ears of everyone. Then it began to

Before the rain had hardly stopped falling, they were out in the mealie lands, planting and singing for joy.

rain—gently at first, with giant drops that made big plops in the thick dust. Then it began to pour, but the thirsty ground drank it as fast as it came down for quite a while. People were so happy that they ran right out into the rain and let it beat against their faces and arms and hands.

Everybody searched out seeds. Before the rain had hardly stopped falling, they were out in the mealie lands, planting and singing for joy. God does answer prayer. He does! He does! And Roy John knows it for himself, just as Tsoka found it out for himself years and years before.

Ntupanyama's School Register

BODY of an animal." That is what Ntupanyama means. Yes, African mothers, especially the heathen ones, name their babies queer names indeed. Often they name them bad names, thinking that in this way they will deceive the evil spirits which might come and make their children sick.

If the evil spirit should say, "What is this child's name?" and the parents should answer, "Wakufakalekale," they think the evil spirit is likely to say, "Oh, it is no use to stay around here," for Wakufakalekale means "he died a long time ago."

Many African boys and girls, when they get just a little older, notice that most people have two names, so more than likely they will choose other names. Sometimes, if they are not wise, they choose names that make people laugh— like Kidney, or Abscess, or Strawberry Jam. Ntupanyama chose the name Kennedy for his first name, and after that he always told people he was Kennedy Ntupanyama. He was born in a village named Msambanjati, which means "the bath place for the buffalo."

Kennedy went to school at the Tekerani Mission Station. Because of the great shortage of teachers, the older boys often went out in the afternoon to teach in the small village schools. This was hard, for these boys had not had a bit of training to teach, and some of them did not make good teachers.

Still it was felt that a poor teacher is better than no teacher at all. But there were certain rules that the mission director laid down for these young men to follow. One of them was in regard to the school register. You see, most of these boys had never owned anything valuable in all their lives; it was hard for them to learn to take care of things. This was a lesson the white *bwana* wanted to teach them.

Because paper is expensive in central Africa, small notebooks and pieces of paper must never be wasted, but must be used to a good advantage. "Take good care of your register," the *bwana* told the boys who went out to teach. "Do not tear it, drop it, or let it get dirty. And I am sorry to tell you that if you lose it or ruin it, you will have to pay a fine, for these registers are all supposed to be turned in to the director of education in Zomba."

At first Kennedy went to teach in a small school in the village of Tambizi. The little children loved him, and they were happy learning, working, and playing together. But one day the mission director called Kennedy.

"Ntupanyama," he said, "I am having a little trouble over at the Zilima school. I have been thinking it over, and I think I will put you at Zilima and take the teacher who is there and give him your school. There are some big troublesome boys who are giving this other teacher a lot of cheek. I believe you can handle the situation."

It warmed Kennedy's heart to know that the *bwana* believed in him, but he hated the thought of leaving his sweet little school at Tambizi. He had everything organized, and the children were doing well. That evening the young teacher came to Kennedy's house and brought him the Zilima register.

"I have come to bring and to take," he laughed. "To bring the register of Zilima and to take the one for Tambizi. My, but I am glad to make the change. That is a hard school, and I feel sorry for you. There are about eight boys who will not do as I tell them to do, and cause trouble all the time."

"I will get you the Tambizi register right now," said Kennedy. "I left it with my other books right there on the table."

He went over to the table confident that he could pick it up right away, for he thought it was lying on the top of the pile of books. But it was not there. Still he was not worried; he remembered distinctly bringing it home, for he knew it would be the last time he would need it at Tambizi.

It was not on the top, so he went through the pile of books, thinking he must have put it under some of the things, though he did not remember that he had. It was not there. Then he got frantic and moved everything on the table—every book, every notebook. He knew it had been there, for as he laid it down, he noted a tiny ink blot beside the name Tambizi. He had comforted himself that the blot had been there when the book was given to him.

"Can't you find it?" asked the other teacher sympathetically. "That is too bad. But you will find it," he added. "I will stop by for it tomorrow."

When he left, Kennedy dropped to his knees and began to pray with all his heart. He knew he had not been careless with the register, for he had taken care every day to see that he had it before he went to school and when he came home. There is no place in African schools to leave supplies and books, since there are no doors or windows, and in some places people steal everything they can lay their hands on.

"Please help me to find it, dear God," he prayed. "Please help me. I am too poor to pay that big fine, and I want the *bwana* to continue to trust me."

Then he got up and went through everything again. He had other things he needed to do, but he was so worried over the register that he could not get down to anything until he found it. That register simply was not there with his things. Could it be that some of the neighbor children had come in when he was not looking and taken it? Then he noticed that the wind was blowing in the door quite hard. Hope sprang up in his heart. That was it. It had likely blown off the table. He went over the whole hut. Along the wall was a seat made of bricks and plastered over with mud. Hopelessly he peered down into the dusty crack between the bricks and the mud wall. There it was. The wind, by some crazy quirk, had swooped it up and sailed it down into the crack as if it had been edged in by hand.

With the register in his hands he dropped to his knees again and thanked the Lord for the answer to his prayer. His honor, his reliability, were safe. And a great weight rolled off his heart.

Before Livingstone Went to Africa

L ONG, long ago, we learn from the old people who are still alive, the country of Nyasaland in Africa was just rolling bush land. Many an African village was huddled in dense thickets or perched on high tablelands of the mountains, for there was much to fear in those days. If a man went to the waterside, he was not at all sure of returning; slavers might catch him and sell him. He might have to march across the burning sands to Zanzibar, the name of which struck terror to the simple people's hearts. Or he might be bitten by a poisonous snake or eaten by a lion or a leopard. Oh, all the old people agree, especially those who remember the tales of their parents and grandparents, that those were terrible days.

About one hundred and fifty miles south of lovely Lake Nyasa the Nambichamba River leaps over a scenic rocky drop and forms the lovely Nsuadzi Falls. Few people appreciated the falls until comparatively recent years, for no one thought of beauty in days when mere existence was an everyday problem. Beyond the falls the merry little river flows onward many miles, meandering over and around gigantic boulders and through bush so dense that the stream is in twilight all day. Off in the distance, like an eternal watchman, Mt. Mlanje has sat unperturbed through the ages since the great Flood. Clouds form jaunty headdresses, and angry thunderheads beat out futile anger against her stubborn sullen crags. And there are people who offer sacrifices to this mountain and worship it.

If a person could have walked through the dense bush in that far-off day, he would have wondered, Where *is* everybody? Where are the men and the women and the little children? But they were there. Tiny huts, almost like playhouses, snuggled close to giant mahogany trees. Sparse gardens were scratched in fertile soil by a harrassed people who knew all too well their own danger.

About fifteen miles from tall, cone-shaped Cholo Mountain and sixty miles from Mlanje was a small village named Tsapa. It was near the Nambichamba, for the people dared not go far for water and bathing in those days. Poor little village. The people lived in constant fear of a slave raid. They were so hidden and so small that they were seldom found. An old chief later said:

"We of Tsapa and Mbalanguzi, the next village, used to run to Cholo Mountain to hide from the slavers when they came through the country stealing people and cattle. We always kept food hidden in a place we had chosen to hide. But when we crept back home again, usually our houses were burned, our crops ruined, and our animals stolen. We had to rebuild Tsapa and Mbalanguzi again and again. Those were very bad days, very, very bad indeed. The children and young people of today do not know how good these days are."

In this small village of Tsapa, long ago, there lived a strong, good native man named Kasonga. He was not a Christian, of course, for he had never heard that blessed name. A great writer once said:

"Even among the heathen are those who have cherished the spirit of kindness. Before the words of life have fallen upon their ears, they have befriended missionaries, even ministering to them at the peril of their own lives. Among the heathen are those who worship God ignorantly, those to whom the light is never brought by human instrumentality, yet they will not perish. Though ignorant of the written law of God, they have heard His voice speaking to them in nature, and have done the things that the law required. Their works are evidence that the Holy Spirit has spoken to their hearts, and they are recognized as children of God."—*Desire of Ages,* p. 638.

Kasonga was such a man. He was known among his villagers as one who was fair and good. People brought disputes to him to decide and problems of life to solve. They depended on him. He was tall, with strong, muscular arms and legs, and an almost Indianlike countenance. Under the brown skin his muscles rippled, and his firm, square jaw and burning eyes set deep showed ardent determination. His loin cloth was made of the bark of a tree and beaten into a clothlike softness.

At the place where his hut was built was a great flat stone, almost as big as the floor of a room. It was buried in the ground until only the smooth surface lay there white and clean. His young wife, Noliti, used to pound her mealies for porridge and spread the meal out on this big stone to dry. She was glad she had that stone, and she used to brag about it to her fellow villagers just as people nowadays are proud of freezers and automatic washing machines.

"I have that wonderful stone near to my hut," she used to say joyfully. "It is not necessary for me to lay *ngaiwa* out on mats. I just spread it out on that stone."

Of course some of the women were a little jealous, yet

she was so sweet they could not be very angry, for she always told them to come and use the wonderful stone too.

"*Malo zakwana!*" she'd say, smiling happily. "There is room enough."

There at Tsapa village the mealies grew on the hillsides, for the village was built on a hill that led down to the bank of the river. Beans climbed the stalks of the mealies, and pumpkins ripened there. When the corn had dried in the shucks, the women shelled it and pounded it into meal as they needed it.

Naked babies rolled and played in the dirt of the courtyard, and bigger children chased the monkeys and baboons out of the mealie fields. The lions, leopards, and hyenas frightened the simple village folk at nighttime, so the villagers took the fowls and the goats right into the houses, or they all would have been eaten.

But the greatest, the most horrible fear of all was of the slavers, who crept through the bush like evil shadows and caught people to sell in the slave market at Zanzibar. Village after village had been wiped out by these devils in human form.

Little Tsapa and Mbalanguzi were saved time and again. The people in these villages were near enough to the Dambo Escarpment Cliffs where the slavers often crept in, so that they could see the flames of burning Nyodola and Kaipsa and hear the screams of the people there. There never was a moment to spare; they had learned by bitter experience to pick up and flee for their lives on a moment's notice.

When the slavers would arrive, the people, the fowls, and some of the small animals would all be gone, even though the fires would still be burning in the kitchen huts and food scorching in the clay pots. The people came this close to being caught many, many times.

But one terrible day little Tsapa and Mbalanguzi were caught. And one of those who was caught and bound was Kasonga—strong, good Kasonga. He was wild with anger and sorrow to see his small wife bound and taken in one direction. Fighting futilely to the last, he screamed in agony as she disappeared into the bush. Before she had gone far, she turned and looked at him and cried out, *"Tsalani Bwino,"* while she caught at the rough ropes tied too tightly around her smooth neck.

Kasonga was subdued roughly with kicks and blows until he lay quite quiet. Then the slavers fastened a tough forked stick called a *gori* on his neck and gave him a great load of ivory to carry on his head. He had not been allowed to answer his pretty one, his lost Noliti, for they had thrown him to the ground and kicked him in the face about then. When he looked up later, the trees stood as they had, but the long line of slaves had passed on and out of his life forever. Some people thought that the black man could not feel sorrow. They thought he could get over agonies, indignities, insults, and injustices quickly. But this is not true. In the wonderful book that the angels keep, all these things are faithfully recorded, for the Judge of all the earth cannot do evil. And the crimes that have been committed, man against man, will be met one day at the judgment bar of God.

When Kasonga and all those of his slave gang were securely fastened together and driven away, he took one last despairing look at Tsapa. There was his little hut. He could smell the *nsima* burning in the little cook hut that Noliti had put on for their dinner. In the midst of the great flat white stone was *ngaiwa* spread out to dry by Noliti's quick hands. Now the birds and the rats and the lizards would eat it. And the bush would creep in with its constant growing, growing, growing and would swallow up his house and his garden and the whole village. He thought in despair, "I will never, never see Tsapa any more. Never."

Terrible sobs wrenched his body. Tears burst from his eyes and rained down his cheeks. He was not ashamed, for every man in the long line was weeping and moaning.

But his tough bare feet found the path, and numbly he balanced his heavy load of ivory on his head. There was nothing else to do. Nothing. The arms and the strength were all on the side of the captors. He could hear behind him and ahead of him the shouts of the slavers and the singing whine of the long cruel whips as they cut the blood out of some poor stumbler's back. Dumb with mental and physical agony, the gang covered the miles.

And how beautiful had been this morning, thought Kasonga. There had been a dew that spangled the grasses, and the first maize was almost ready to eat. In one more week he and Noliti would have been roasting the corn, delicious and tender, the grains puffy with milk. The sunlight had come over the mountains in bright banners. He had been at work early and had eaten a tender *pwepwete* when he heard Noliti's scream. Now all that was just a memory.

Many of every slave gang died in the fearful march to the sea. Fever, hunger, thirst, weakness, and harsh treatment took its toll; many fell by the wayside. To discourage those who might feign sickness, the slavers tied the poor sufferers to the ground, so they could not defend themselves against the wild beasts that were sure to find them. If babies or small children cried or got sick or in any way troubled the *akapolo,* they were torn from their mothers' backs and thrown into the bush to perish.

After many weeks Kasonga, with the others who had sur-

139

vived the gruelling march, arrived at a place on the Indian Ocean called Bwani. He did not have any way of knowing what would happen to him. Would he be put into an Arab boat and taken out to the slave block on the Spice Island of Zanzibar? If that was to be his lot, he well knew that he would be sold and taken away on a huge boat to some far-away land, and never again would he see the shores of his native land. Never again would he see the purple slopes of Mlanje, the thundering falls at Nsuadzi, or the hum of life as he knew it at Tsapa village.

He did not know how to pray, for Kasonga did not know God. But he had heard the voice of God speaking in nature, and he had in his simple and childlike way done the things the law required. God was watching while he waited and hoped.

The gall of slavery was less bitter when he learned that he had been sold to Makalanjira, a rich Yao, who dealt in ivory, ebony, and the souls of men. His wealth was gotten in great wickedness—in war, in pillage, and in laying waste. For such there will be a just reward.

Kasonga's work for Makalanjira was the work of gardening. This was more pleasing to him than if he had been taken on the raiding expeditions which brought in such wealth. Among the growing plants and the flowers and shrubs his master's wife loved, he found a kind of peace. In the long hours of digging, carrying water, transplanting, sowing, and then reaping, he began to hope; for hope springs eternal in the human heart. He had long known the meaning of great patience, and he knew that years must elapse before he would dare try to get away.

Even though he was diligent, silent, and tireless in his work, he could never satisfy Malisao, the head boss. Kasonga's back was often cruelly lacerated by the buffalo whip when he had no idea what he had done or left undone. A kind of tragic hopelessness began to possess him, until he began to think about killing himself.

He bore all his injustices silently. But when his night seemed the darkest, a brightness came in which almost blinded him at first. The wife of the cruel owner came into the garden one day when Malisao had given Kasonga a cruel cut with the whip.

"Malisao, what did this man do that you should beat him in this way?" she asked quietly.

"He-he-he-he is lazy. He will not work."

The wife stood looking at Malisao for a moment; then she said in a quiet voice, "Very well. If he is so bad and so lazy, let me keep him under my close supervision. I will have him work in my kitchen garden, and with my flowers, and with the plants in my dooryard."

And to Kasonga's deep, undying joy, he was taken from the field and from under the brutal tyranny of Malisao.

Kasonga was more scrupulous than ever, and he also noted that Malisao was taken from his work in a few days. He knew that the wife had given bad reports to her husband about Malisao's work. Later Kasonga saw him working in the fields along with the other slaves.

The master's wife was as kind to Kasonga as she dared to be. When her fierce husband was gone on one of his many expeditions, she would come with bread, bananas, and milk and give them to the half-starved slaves. She had kind words for them, too, which they needed more than food and drink. Her voice was soft and kind and trembling with more pity than she dared reveal.

The poor slaves understood. She helped cover up some of their fumbling mistakes and saved them many a beating. But she took a special liking to Kasonga.

"Kasonga," she said kindly one day while he was digging in her flower beds, "I see a look in your eyes I do not see in the eyes of the other slaves. It is an unbeaten and unconquered look. Oh, Kasonga, be careful. Be careful. My husband has one sentence for those who try to run away. And you know what that is."

Kasonga knew. Death. And not a quick death. A long, hard death. He looked up at the gray-haired woman in astonishment. "And can mamma read the thoughts that are locked up inside my head?" he asked quietly.

"Your eyes are windows, Kasonga," she replied. "And sometimes I can see into those windows and see things that scare me. I fear for you. I tremble for you. Your life is precious. It does not belong to you or to my husband. It belongs to the great God."

"To the great God, madam? And who and where is He? He must not be the god of the black man, for who has more troubles than we? It is plain that no Great One cares for us. No Great One listens to our cries. We are as dung upon the ground."

The gentle woman looked up from the bit of sewing she was doing.

"These things that you are reasoning are not true, Kasonga. Little by little I will tell you of God and of Jesus Christ, His Son. Jesus, the Son, made Himself into a man and lived here on this earth and suffered as much at the hands of cruel men as you do, Kasonga. But I cannot tell it all to you now. But you must know."

Kasonga pondered this. It was hard to believe that God could suffer as he had, but because the good woman had told him, he knew it must be true.

"Kasonga," she spoke again, "your country must be beautiful. The sadness and the longing have never dimmed in your eyes all these years that you have been at Bwani."

Then Kasonga wept aloud as he told her of the leaping little river, of the Nsuadzi Falls, of Cholo Mountain with its green forests, of Tsapa, and of Mt. Mlanje in the far distance. And he told her of gay, singing Noliti, his girl wife, who kept the big flat stone swept clean.

"You will never find your Noliti," replied the good woman after a while. "But I asked my husband last week to let me find a wife for you. He consented. I am going to give you Ndamvelekina. You have seen her. She works in my house and keeps the clothing mended and in order. She will be a good wife to you, Kasonga. She was caught in an expedition of my husband several years ago. She came here on her mother's back, but the mother had the fever and died in a few days. She does not remember any life other than a life of slavery."

"She must be a Mang'anja of my tribe, madam, for her name is a Mang'anja word. Do you know what Ndamvelekina means, madam?"

"Why, no, Kasonga; I do not know. What does it mean?"

Kasonga smiled as happily as he had smiled in all the years of his captivity. It made him warm inside to remember his native tongue that had lain sleeping in his heart.

"It means 'I heard something else,' " he answered softly. "And today I have heard something else, such good words, that are medicine to my sick heart. Maybe there are brighter days someplace in the future for me—a day when I might be able to laugh again. I have almost forgotten laughter."

"Yes, oh, yes, Kasonga," answered the good woman. "We hope for brighter days." When she leaned toward him and whispered softly, "Someday I will help you and Ndamvelekina escape, but we must wait for the proper time; and, Kasonga, you will see your Tsapa again."

Looking into the eyes of the kind woman, Kasonga saw the light of God, a brightness, a glow that defies all description, and a wild joyful hope sprang up into his poor heart.

Time dragged on; but Kasonga was happier now because Ndamvelekina was his wife. Almost a year had gone by. It was late at night, and he had just finished his evening meal. He had been late because he had worked late, helping his master prepare for another marauding expedition, as he had done many, many times in the past. This time he had dozens of slaves—miserable, silent creatures—fastened in a dirty kraal. He had the dhows and was taking them to Zanzibar to the slave market. Then Kasonga and Ndamvelekina heard the matting at their door rattle.

"Who is it?" whispered Kasonga in great fear. The door

The door mat was pushed aside quickly,
and there stood the master's kind wife.

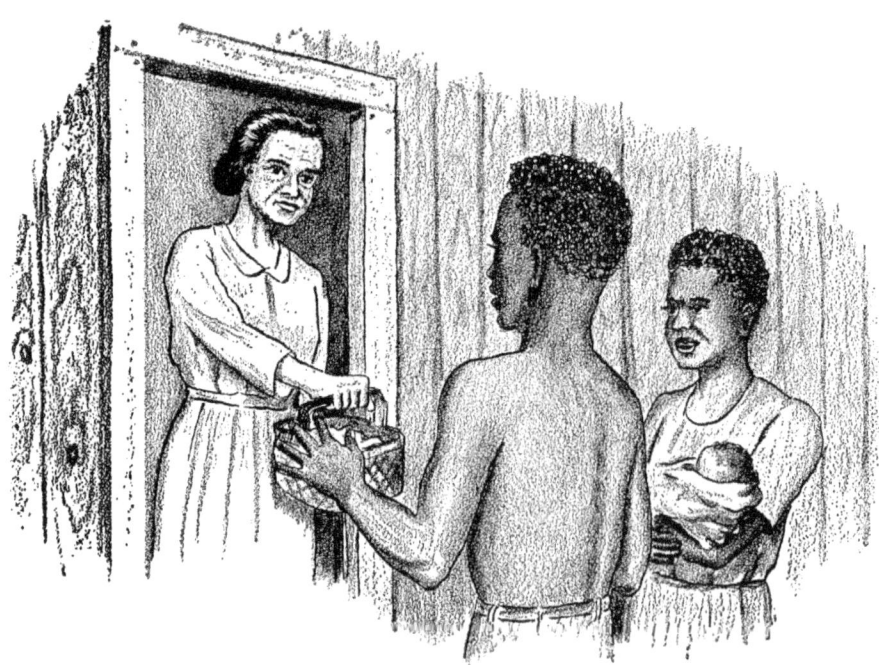

mat was pushed aside quickly, and there stood the master's wife, her face a lighter patch in the dim light.

"Quick! Quick!" she breathed. "Go . . . and go now . . . you, too, Ndamvelekina. My husband plans to take you both to Zanzibar in the morning. I was wakeful and got up and saw the lists on the table. Oh, don't worry; he has so much rum inside him now he will never know I left the house. He is sleeping like a fat pup. He will not blame me, for I am not supposed to have read the lists. I never do. But here . . . leave everything. This is food . . . some money, some salt for trading, and a small gun. Do not allow yourselves to be caught." And she handed Kasonga a tightly packed basket. She fairly shoved the two of them out into the night.

"Go now. Go, and God be with you," she sobbed. And the night closed in around the two fugitives. Into the blackness of the night Kasonga and Ndamvelekina crept. On Ndamvelekina's back, tied in a goatskin, was a tiny black babe only days old. The madam had named him—a name from God's Book—Amos.

When danger is great—so great that life itself is at stake—sometimes people can walk without fear, with a clearness of purpose and a determination that spell victory. Kasonga, with primitive accuracy, knew the general direction. He had a bow and many arrows in his quiver, which he understood better than the small gun his mistress had given him. He had a razor-sharp spear and a knobkerrie club he had made himself. Ndamvelekina carried her babe on her back and the basket on her head.

Swiftly they trod the paths that Kasonga knew very well. Through the years he had gone this way with his master. He knew well that at daybreak, not many hours hence, swift, cruel men would be sent to recapture him and his

10   145

wife. They would conclude that they could not travel far, since Ndamvelekina's baby was very young. Because of this, Kasonga went due south instead of westward as he knew they would expect him to do. He had heard of a cave in a mountain, and there he was wending his footsteps. There he would hide with his wife and babe until the trail grew cold. Then he would travel only at night.

It was wise that he did, for his pursuers did just as he expected them to do, but returned at night spent and angry —and without the runaways. After three months of hiding by day and walking by night, Kasonga sensed that he must be getting onto familiar ground. He was filled with excitement and joy. One bright dawn, when they were in what Kasonga thought must be the mountains of his native land, he caught sight of the purple grandeur of a mighty mountain. He was ahead in the path, and he gave one look and then cried out with a loud voice.

Ndamvelekina ran to him in great fright.

"What? What? What?" she cried with great fear.

"It is Mlanje . . . Mlanje . . . Mlanje, the mountain which we saw every day from Tsapa. We are near . . . near . . . near. We are near to the village where I was born, and where my fathers have all lived and died!"

Then he threw himself down and caressed and patted the soil and the rough grasses by the pathway. He would have kissed the ground again and again if he had known what a kiss means.

It was only the matter of another part of a day now. By nightfall Ndamvelekina, Kasonga, and tiny Amos had crossed the dimpling Nambichamba River. At every step of the way Kasonga grew more deliriously happy. He would have been happier yet if he had known that slavery was dying. He did not know that the slavers were coming more and more seldom. The world was waking up to what had been happening; the twentieth century was just around the corner. Good men, whose convictions were hallowed and sanctified by prayer and righteous living, had put a stop to this unholy traffic.

Then they came to the great stone, the flat floor which had been Noliti's pride and joy. He could hardly wait for another day when he could begin. Then he heard a sound. An old woman crept fearfully through the bush, peering curiously at Kasonga and Ndamvelekina. Looking at her closely, Kasonga suddenly sprang into the air for very joy.

"Amai! Amai!" he shouted, tears streaming down his cheeks.

It was indeed his poor old mother, who, alone of all his family, had escaped. She had escaped because she had been at the stream garden when the *akapolo* arrived.

Several years later a Christian mission was established right where Tsapa had been. Kasonga was an old, old man at the time. Kasonga, in his old age, became an ardent Christian. He moved his house to a nearby village, where he lived out his years.

I have lived in the mission house near to the flat stone which was Noliti's pride and joy. I dried corn meal on that old flat stone, too.

People have forgotten where they laid the bones of old Kasonga and Ndamvelekina his wife. But the Lord knows, and He will raise them up in the last day. They were faithful unto death, and surely they deserve and will receive the crown of life.

Strange African Stories

WHEN bedtime comes in Africa, the little children are not tucked into clean beds such as you have. And the mothers do not sit down by the beds and tell them stories such as you hear. But the little African children hear and enjoy stories just the same—strange stories. And they are told in the shadow of a mud hut, around a blazing fire. The light flickers in the wondering black faces of the children as the old uncle or grandfather tells many strange stories.

There is one story which reminds me of a story in the Bible. Can you tell what it is?

Long, long ago there lived a rich chief in his fine village. A beautiful river ran through it, and there were bright fish of many kinds in its clear waters. But the people were afraid of their great chief. His voice was loud, and people ran when they heard him. And no matter what the chief wanted, the people tried to get it for him to keep him in good humor.

One night the chief sat in his cattle kraal and looked out at the brilliant night sky. There was the moon like a giant circle of gold. "That is a piece of gold cloth hanging up there in the sky," the chief suddenly said. Then he began to

The light flickers in the black faces as the
old uncle or grandfather tells the stories.

shout and jump up and down. "I want to have that piece
of gold cloth to make me a new coat," he thundered.

The people were frightened. The next day they began to
build a tower. They said that they would build it high
enough to reach the moon. Then their chief could have the
moon to cut up and make into a coat.

They built and built and toiled and labored for weeks
and months and years, but they never did get the tower
high enough to reach the moon. Did you ever hear a story
something like that?

There is another story that the little children love to hear:

Long ago the great God asked the black men if they
would like to be white again and go to live in the white
man's land. All the Africans said, "Yes, yes," they would be
glad to be white.

149

Then they were told to go to the waters of a great river which was flowing in the north, and bathe themselves. And then they were to wade across this river to the white man's land, and there they would live happily. All the Africans went to the banks of the great river. Some went in and were made white. They crossed the river happily and were heard of no more. They had gone to the white man's land.

Most of the Africans said, "We are very tired tonight. We will sleep here by the side of the river, and tomorrow or the next day we will go across."

But the old story goes that the next morning when they awoke, the river was gone. There was only a trickle of water running through the sandy river bed.

With moans of sorrow the Africans sprang forward and tried to get into the precious water. But all they could do was to get the soles of their feet and the palms of their hands wet. And that is why, the old chiefs like to tell, Africans have white palms and soles.

Of course that is not a true story, but it shows you what kind of tales the African children hear around the flickering fires.

Then the grandpa tells the children that he knows why the hen always is scratching in the ground, and why she always runs when she sees a chicken hawk.

Old black Bombo chuckles a little when he tells this story:

Long ago the hawk lent the hen her needle. The hen wanted the needle so she could sew her wings and make them look beautiful. But before she ever got to use it, Mrs. Hen lost the fine needle which the hawk had let her have.

"Now just watch the hen," the old man says to the children. "Can't you see her scratching, scratching in the ground looking always for the needle? Then when the hawk comes down, the hen runs, for she has not found the needle."

The old man pauses. "And do you know what the hawk says when he swoops down? He says, 'You better run, you bad old hen. I will take you away and eat you, because you have lost my needle.'"

It is strange, but Africans do not like the chameleon. It is a harmless little creature, but the children will run if they see it on a mossy stone or in a bush or tree. This is the story that is told around the fires about the little chameleon:

Long years ago, when the earth was young, God saw that men were sad because there was death in the earth. So God said to the chameleon, "You go down to the earth and tell men that though they die, they will live again." But the little chameleon was a lazy creature and played along the road. He did not care how much men sorrowed and how much men wept—just so he could play and have a happy time.

The evil one saw that the chameleon was playing by the way and not obeying the voice of God. So he laughed and said, "I too will send a messenger." So he called a lizard to him and said, "You go to the earth and take a message. Tell them that death is eternal sleep. No one can ever come back from the grave. They are gone forever." The lizard ran fast to the earth. He spread his message of sorrow everywhere. The whole earth was plunged in despair. Cries of anguish went up from humanity.

A long time later the little chameleon came to earth. "If you die, you will live again," he told the people. But they would not believe him. "You came too late. We have been told that there is no hope. How can we believe you?"

That is the reason, so the Africans say, that they all hate the chameleon.

Boys and girls, are you a chameleon or a swift little

lizard? Do you hurry to obey, or do you play along the road? The lizard obeyed the voice of Satan quickly. Satan is not a good master. How much more quickly should we obey the commands of our kind, loving Saviour or our earthly parents who are so good to us!

Johnnie Baboon Goes to Church

DEVIR and Bonnie bought Johnnie the baboon from a tall native boy who worked at the police station six miles from the mission. The boy said he was gentle and harmless, but he was far from being either one. True, he did not want to hurt anyone at first, but he destroyed things all the time. He chased the chickens, mauled the cats, and scared the dogs.

He loved to get up on the porch and throw all the flowerpots off onto the ground. What mother would like that? No, not even a missionary mother. So the children's mother was firm. Johnnie must be tied, and kept tied. At first he spent all his time trying to pull up the stake or bite the chain in two. Then he got cross and ferocious. He would show his teeth every time Bonnie and Devir came near. Only their mother could go near him and feed him.

He would eat the bananas and papayas she brought; then he'd lie down for her to scratch his stomach. How he loved that! He would lie flat on his back, happy as could be as long as he was being petted.

But a missionary mother has other things to do than scratch baboons. One Friday she said firmly, "Sunday Johnnie has to go back to the police station to his other owner. He is a bother and a nuisance, and I do not want him around the house any more."

Devir and Bonnie did not care much, for he was no fun any more since he had gotten so cross and ugly. The next morning when the children were getting ready to go to church, Devir noticed that Johnnie was gone—chain, stake, and all.

"Mother! Johnnie is gone!" he shouted excitedly.

"Oh, my peas and my flowers!" cried mother.

Devir went flying to the garden, but was relieved to see that Johnnie had not been there.

There was no sign of Johnnie by nine o'clock, so they all went to church. Sabbath school went along fine. The native children recited their memory verses, looked at the picture roll, and sang, "Rock, Rock, Rock," in their native tongue so full of "z's" and "ng's."

Then church service began. The babies were asleep on their mothers' backs, and the little children were wriggling on the pews like rows of black tumblebugs.

They had just sung a song:

"Poyang'ana Yesuyo, Pa kuona mtandawo
Tingapeze moyowo, Poyang'ana Yesuijo."

To that same tune you'd sing, "There's life in a look." But the native children sang it as lustily as you do.

Just then a terrible commotion began in the back of the church. Johnnie had come flying merrily through the window. He jumped on the women's shoulders and heads. The women screamed. Then the babies woke up and shrieked, and the whole church was a bedlam in a minute.

But Johnnie was enjoying himself immensely. The deacons had to do something; so, armed with sticks, they approached him cautiously. Johnnie sailed out through the window and up the nearest tree. The good black deacons hurried to lock and bolt the shutters. The church was plunged in darkness, but at least there was some peace and quiet. Every window was fastened securely, but one had the hasp broken off. So they propped it shut with a board and hoped that Johnnie wouldn't notice it.

But his sharp eyes took in everything. They no sooner had gone back into the church than Johnnie was rattling violently at the loose window shutter. No one could hear a thing. Rattle, rattle, clatter, bang, with Johnnie's high chatter as a funny accompaniment.

Suddenly the window gave way, and the hairy, mischievous face of Johnnie peered in at the window. Then mother went outside and succeeded in capturing Johnnie. The rest of the service droned on while mother sat on the grass and scratched Johnnie's stomach.

A boy was sent to the police station to get Johnnie's former owner, and a little while later Johnnie rode merrily away, fastened to the back tandem of the native policeman's bicycle.

And perhaps that's where naughty Johnnie ought to be— at the police station, for it is a very, very bad thing to break up a church service.

The Story of Nyra

THE DOCTOR'S three little children were sound asleep in their white beds in the mission cottage. The sun beat down fiercely. It had not rained for a long time, and the air was full of dust and dirt.

The doctor had just sat down to rest a few moments before he went down to the dispensary to begin his long afternoon of work. This was the hot season, and many black children were sick with fevers or sores. Fathers and mothers were sick, too, and old people moaned with illness in the villages. They were all hungry, for there was a famine in the land. The plants would not grow in the dry fields, and the grass was as dry as straw. Day after day went by, and still it did not rain. Every day starving people came to the mission house and begged for food.

There was one thing that the mother had grown in her garden that year. It was pumpkins—hundreds of them. The doctor's children ate them every day for months. Perhaps while you were whining that you got tired of oatmeal and orange juice for breakfast, Nell and Lois and Donnie were glad to have baked pumpkin with a little honey on it. Perhaps while you complained that you never could like creamed carrots and spinach, they were sitting down to a meal of boiled pumpkin, and glad to get it. Your bowls of dry cereal and milk would have looked good to them. I think they would have gladly traded you their little dish of pumpkin sauce for it.

They tried to have a proper garden and wet it with water from the well, but at night starving people would pull up the tender pea vines and eat them ravenously, or pluck off the growing pineapples long before they were ripe.

On this particular day the doctor heard a little commotion out in front of his house. He hurried out onto the porch to see what it was all about. What a sight met his eyes! There stood a tall, strong heathen chief with a magnificent leopard skin wrapped around his glistening black body. By his side was a poor little girl clad in filthy rags. She was holding out her little scrawny arms pitifully to the doctor. Her black hands were badly burned. The doctor could see in a moment that nothing could be done to save her hands.

What had happened to little Nyra Chumagufi's hands? I will tell you, and then I am sure you will be glad that you have a Christian mother to take care of you and love you.

Little Nyra had a terrible mother. She did not have the love of God in her heart, and her soul was as black as her skin. She believed in the awful superstitions of devil worship, so she did not even love her own little girl. She did not love anyone but herself.

When the famine came into the land, the wicked woman kept all the food she found for herself and her mean old uncle. Day after day passed, and Nyra would see them eating, but they would not let her have one bite. Day after day Nyra would search the barren bush for food, weeping and crying from hunger. Finally she was just a living skeleton, hardly able to move about. Her hands looked like the black claws of a bird.

One evening Nyra crept out of the hut when she thought that neither her mother nor her uncle was watching her. She crept noiselessly over to the poor, dry, cracked garden where a few potato vines were creeping over the powdery ground. She pulled away a piece of vine and crammed it into her mouth and began to chew it quickly. How hungry she was! How good this dusty piece of vine tasted! She felt as if she could eat all the vines in this garden and still feel starved.

Just then she fell to the ground in terrible fear. A wild shout from the hut told her that her wicked mother had discovered her. Then poor little Nyra was seized roughly and dragged screaming into the cook hut. The angry woman built a great fire in one corner. Nyra watched the red glow in awful fear. What was her mother going to do to her?

About that time the mother pulled her little girl to the fire and held her black hands against the red coals. The girl screamed till she fainted away. Then, as if that were not enough, the bad woman drove the girl out into the bush and would not allow her in the hut all night. It's awful to think that a mother could be so cruel to her own daughter, but Satan ruled her heart.

While you had such a nice clean bed that night, and while you had such a good, kind mother, little Nyra wandered in the bush, holding her burned little hands in front of her and weeping wildly. God must have protected her from the hungry leopards and lions that night. The chief found her soon after that, and even his heathen heart was touched by her suffering and need. He took her to the mission station as fast as he could go.

The first thing they did was to bandage her terrible burns. Then they began to give her food. She ate like a ravenous little beast, scooping the food up even with the sore band-

The chief found her soon after that, and even his heathen heart was touched by her suffering and need.

aged stubs of arms. It seemed to the doctor's wife that she never, never could get little Nyra full. At one meal she ate an oatmeal tin of sour milk, another of peas, and several bananas.

While she was lying in the hospital, someone made her a rag doll. Tears sprang into Nyra's eyes. She seized the poor rag thing, pressed it to her heart, and began to weep aloud. It was the first pretty thing she had ever had in all her life.

Now Nyra is going to the mission school. She can dress herself and even eat with her stubs of arms. You should see her hold an ear of corn with her elbows.

Someday, soon, our precious Saviour will come in the clouds of heaven. Then, little Nyra—if she continues to be a good, faithful girl—will have hands again; for she, too, will be changed "in a moment, in the twinkling of an eye, at the last trump."

Katundu and the Lion

NOT MANY years ago there lived in northern Nyasaland a little boy named Katundu. He was a heathen boy at the time and knew nothing about Sabbath school, or church, or even good clothing.

One day Katundu's father called to him. "You, my son, come here!"

Katundu ran quickly to his father's side. "What is it, Bambo?" the small boy asked. Bambo means "father" in Katundu's language.

"You are old enough now to go and help herd the cows and goats. It is not good for you to play all day long. You must begin now to be a little man." Katundu was glad to hear this, for he was eager to grow up and be a man.

The next morning Katundu bravely set forth with the others toward the grassy pasture. He carried some bananas and a boiled sweet potato to eat when he got hungry. All the boys were happy. But there was one thing that wasn't good. No shepherd boy was allowed to cut his hair. The fathers and mothers told the boys that some great disaster would happen to their flocks and herds if they cut off their thick, fuzzy hair. It was a strange superstition, but they all believed it. So every one of the boys was tormented with lice, and they were constantly scratching and digging at their heads to get rid of the lice. Because of this their scalps were covered with scabs.

After Katundu had been with the cattle about a month, he felt quite at home with his new work. He knew how to run around the herd shouting and waving a bamboo stick if the humpbacked cattle wandered too far away.

One day while the boys were watching the animals, Katundu's father and some hunters came through the bush.

"A lion was in yonder village last night," the father said. "We are tracking him so we can kill him!" The boys watched the father disappear into the bush, but they had no desire to follow. A lion was too fierce and treacherous. Let father and the hunters catch him, if they wished, for they had great bows and long arrows.

The boys were talking about the hunt and idly watching the grazing cattle when suddenly the bushes parted and a huge lion rushed into the clearing. His eyes gleamed fiercely, and his mane stood straight up. His cruel mouth was open, dripping saliva. The boys froze with terror.

Then Katundu did a foolish thing. He got up and started to run away. Immediately the lion noticed him. With a roar that fairly shook the earth, he bounded after the fleeing child. When the lion was sure of his meal, he gave a long leap, intending to land on Katundu's back and bear him to the ground.

At that moment Katundu stumbled over a root and fell. The lion flew over his head in a gigantic leap, his claws scratching Katundu's back cruelly as he hurtled over.

Poor Katundu thought that his last hour had come. He lay there trembling all over, waiting for the beast to turn and devour him. Presently a strong hand reached down and lifted Katundu.

"Get up, Katundu!" a voice commanded the trembling lad.

"Bambo!"

"Look at the lion, my son!"

Katundu looked. There lay the king of the forest with an arrow piercing his heart. Katundu's father had come just at the right time.

Not long after that an evangelist came to Katundu's village, and the lad and his family heard for the first time the glad story of the soon coming of Jesus. That wonderful new message changed their lives. Then Katundu heard of schools, and right away he wanted to attend. His father and mother found a Seventh-day Adventist school, and soon away went Katundu with his slate and slate pencil.

The school had a mud floor, mud walls, and heaps of dried clay for seats; but Katundu thought it was quite all right. He had never seen a pretty schoolroom such as you know so much about. He hadn't seen a bright picture book or a clean white wall. He had never seen a good table or chair. So he thought nothing of sitting on the floor, writing on a rough slate, and shooing away the green flies that liked to bite his legs. He learned to take a sharp stick and practice writing on the hard clay of the schoolyard, for his school did not have even a blackboard.

After he had passed through four grades, Katundu came to Malamulo Mission. Now he is studying to be a teacher, so he can tell the good news of the kingdom of heaven to someone else.

Katundu believes that he was saved from the "paw of the lion" that he might learn the blessed truth of Christianity. If you are faithful, boys and girls, you will probably meet Katundu in the earth made new. There the lions will be so tame that even a little child can lead them.

Tommy's Prayer

TOMMY lived in a little hut in a village of central Africa. The hut was made of poles laced together with a strong bark string. Then the whole structure was covered with mud. There were no carpets on the floor, not even a piece of linoleum. White ants are so terrible in Africa that even if Tommy's mother had these things, they would not last long. They would soon be eaten to bits. If Tommy left his loincloth on the floor at night, there would be large holes in it by morning.

One evening Tommy's father called him. "Come, my little son, I want to teach you to pray."

This made Tommy happy, for he wanted to learn to pray to God. His father taught his son to say this prayer: "Dear Jesus up in heaven, make me a good boy. Help me to have the Holy Spirit in my life. Help me to chase away all the evil spirits from around our house. Keep me from harm and danger. Amen."

Tommy was so small that he hardly knew what his prayer meant; but because his father had told him he must pray often, he said it many times a day. Sometimes he even stopped his playing to say it.

One day Tommy was all alone in the mud hut. His mother

had asked him to sweep the house for her. Everyone but Tommy had gone to the cornfield to hoe. Because Tommy's family was poor and didn't know better, the hens and roosters and baby chicks came into the house to eat food which the children dropped on the floor. Tommy was sweeping busily in one room and saying his little prayer over and over. Suddenly he heard a noise from the other room.

"Hoosh! Hoosh!" Then he heard the old hen squawk and the baby chicks begin to peep loudly. Tommy ran to the door. There on the floor of the big room was a large snake. It had a baby chicken in its mouth. The others ran away. Just then Tommy's dog ran in, growling, and a puff of wind blew the door shut. Tommy was alone in the house with the dog and the big snake.

Then the snake began to chase Tommy. Poor little boy!

Then the snake began to chase Tommy. Poor little boy! He ran around and around the room.

He ran around and around the room. The dog ran after the snake, biting at its thick body as much as it could. No doubt it helped Tommy.

Then Tommy remembered his prayer, and at that moment his fear left him. He saw in a corner a thick club. He seized this, turned, and hit the snake hard on the head. God helped Tommy to hit it in the right place. When the people came to see the snake, they were frightened. Its head was as big as a man's fist. They were much surprised that a small boy could kill such a ferocious snake. They measured the snake, and it was more than eight feet long.

Tommy told them how he had killed the snake: "God gave me the strength of His arm, and I was able to kill the big snake. That is because I prayed to Him."

Tommy prays often for God to help him to be kind and helpful all through life.

Mitzi

YOU NEVER in your life saw such a cat as Mitzi. She was a lovely black and white kitten when I first got her at the Makwasa Tea Estate in Nyasaland, Africa. I had always loved animals, and I always had at least one pet, if it was nothing but a clucking old hen which followed me everywhere I went.

So Mitzi, tiny, bright-eyed, knew I was her mistress right from the very first. When I came home from school, from teaching the black boys and girls, I could see the tiny little thing running to and fro in the window long before I got to the house. I don't know how she knew I was coming, but even as young as she was, it just seemed as if she could tell time.

Then I would call out, "Mitzi, Mitzi, Mitzi!" and she would lift her tiny body in the air and stand right up to the screen just as if she wanted to fly to me. Oh, she knew me. She knew me and she loved me dearly. She was with me only two days when she came running into the dining room where I was studying, and put her feet up on me to attract my attention. That tiny little thing had a mouse in her dainty mouth, and she wanted me to see it first of all. I was astonished, for she had been weaned for only a few days. After that no mouse dared to show its head or even to nibble ever so secretly. She had it before it could' squeak, "Jack Robinson."

Sandula, the cook boy in the kitchen, liked her, for she never did snatch at things as ill-bred cats had done. She did not get onto the table or up on the shelves, so she won his favor. When he went out in the cool of the afternoon, she used to run to him and creep onto his lap, purring so loudly that it seemed as if there were no muffler on her little motor at all.

Little Koko was my baboon pet, and although Mitzi did not like it very well, Koko sometimes picked her up. But when Koko got interested in searching for fleas, she lay down on the porch all stretched out and relaxed, and Koko had the hunt of her life. She turned back fur and searched and hunted, her hairy little mouth working forty miles an hour all the time. If she found a flea darting through, she would get so excited she would cry out, "Ah-ah-ah-ah" at the top of her voice.

Bonnie Jean Fields was a sweet girl who lived at Matandani Mission. She came to see me one day at Malamulo. Her coming was always a happy occasion. We played with little Mitzi that afternoon and laughed at her funny little antics until we were weak. It was Bonnie Jean who took care of Mitzi when we were away on our coastal furlough. During that time Mitzi had all kinds of bad luck.

Once when she was hunting for rats or lizards, she fell down into a twenty-five-foot-deep cesspool. It looked as though Mitzi were done for then; it did indeed. But Bonnie Jean could not see Mitzi perish in that dirty place, so she and a native girl rigged up a long pole that reached to the bottom of the cesspool.

Mitzi fastened her sharp little claws into the pole and

climbed right out. The two girls then bathed her and set her out in the hot sun to dry, and before the day was over, she was as frisky as ever.

During the six months I was gone, Mitzi grew to be a big cat and had a batch of beautiful kittens. When they were ready to wean, Bonnie learned that I had returned to Malamulo from South Africa. She got ready to send Mitzi back to me, but she wanted to keep the kittens, because they were so pretty.

Her daddy was going to make the trip to Malamulo in his pick-up truck, so Mitzi was put into a large covered basket, and away they went. Of course she did not like the inside of that basket a little bit, or the roar the motor made, or the bouncing and jouncing. I suppose she thought the end of the world was coming to her. After a while the truck struck a bigger bump than usual, and out bounced Mitzi, basket and all, onto the rough ground of the bush road. Luckily the lid bounced off the basket, and Mitzi peered out fearfully. The world had not come to an end. It was still here.

The truck roared on, for Mr. Fields did not know that he had lost an important passenger. But I think Mitzi was glad. She stuck her pretty nose into the air and sniffed. How she could smell that Matandani was in a certain direction all that six miles, I do not know. I do not know that any more than how she could tell time.

But Mitzi started off down the rough road, and with many a disturbed mew decided that she was on the right track. She went as fast as she could. About the time Mitzi got to the outskirts of the mission, Mr. Fields arrived at my mission house.

"Mrs. Edwards, I've got your cat!" he cried.

Well, he *thought* he had. When I ran out to get Mitzi, she was not there. He scratched his head.

169

"Well, what do you know about that?" he asked. "She must have bounced out. I don't have any idea in the world where she is."

About that time the lights went on at Matandani. Bonnie Jean had some of her books and crayons at her table, and she was coloring. Suddenly she heard familiar mews at the door. She looked up. That sounded like Mitzi, but she knew it could not be. Mitzi was at Malamulo by this time. But the mews came again, louder and more insistent. She got up and went to the door. It *was* Mitzi. What in the world had happened! She opened the door, and in she came, limping a little, for six miles is a long way for a little cat.

She quickly lapped up the warm milk Bonnie Jean poured out into a saucer. Then she carefully licked her tired paws and slicked down her dusty coat before she curled up and went to sleep.

At last Mitzi did get to me. I was already in bed, for it was late at night, and I took her into the bedroom and let her out of the big bag. She began to purr loudly as soon as she saw me. Then she went all over the house, investigating every crook and cranny. She did it so wisely and so assuredly that it was plain that she remembered just where she was. I was glad to see Mitzi again for more than one reason. The rats and the mice were beginning to get pestiferous again.

I kept several stalks of bananas in varying stages of ripening hanging on my side porch. Bananas are a cheap and plentiful commodity in central Africa. We eat them every day. The rats could not reach the bananas from the floor, but they got up into my attic someway, then made their way around until they came to the place where the banana ropes were slung over a beam. They slid or climbed down these ropes and had a feast every night. They ruined whole stalks of bananas. I was aggravated at the rascals, but I could not seem to get the better of them.

Mitzi's pretty little nose smelled out the situation right away. She mewed at the door to be let out the very next night. I woke in the night several times to hear the banana ropes squeaking; once I looked out, and a bunch of bananas was swaying back and forth. Those old rats, I thought. They must be bringing camels and elephants to help them!

But the next morning Mitzi was at the door begging to be let in. She looked as though she had put in a night of it, and she *had*. There were several dead rats on the porch, and none had dined on my fat yellow bananas during the night.

Then the news must have been published all over the rat domain that it was exceedingly dangerous to dine on bananas at the home of Mitzi the Mouser. The survivors packed up and left—lock, stock, and barrel. One day while I was searching for something in the garage, I heard movements down in a big cement barrel in a corner of the garage. I went to where Mitzi was sleeping in the sun on the front porch. I picked her up and took her with me to the garage. She purred loudly, delighted as always at human attention. But when we got into the garage, her ears pricked up, and her purrs stopped on a note. She heard what I had heard. I carried her over by the barrel. She peered down in as I held her over the barrel. Suddenly she lunged. She was in and then out of the barrel before I could catch my breath— out with a huge rat in her mouth. Rats moved out of the garage then, as Mitzi moved in.

One night, several months later, I was all alone in my house. My husband had gone to a distant village to hold an effort. I went to sleep to the music of crickets and the tiny, drowsy sounds of the African night.

Suddenly I woke up. Something was on my chest—something wriggly, wettish, and warm. I was so scared I could hardly breathe. I remembered someone telling me about a missionary who woke up in the middle of the night and found that a big snake had decided to spend the night coiled up on his chest. He had to lie there until the morning came and the snake decided to go about his business. I wondered. What could I do? There were no electric lights, and if there had been, I would have been afraid to move lest the creature strike me. I was afraid to reach out and get my flashlight. I was afraid to do anything but lie still while the sweat fairly burst out of my forehead. Then I heard, "Ptrrh, ptrrh," and I knew it was Mitzi. But how did she get wet and wiggly? I was so relieved and so happy I could hardly get my flashlight soon enough. But when I did! When I did!

There was Mitzi. Yes, but she had had five baby kittens on my chest while I was asleep. I did not know I could sleep so soundly!

I got up, found a box, and put the new little family in it, and got them settled right by the side of my bed. Mitzi was purring loudly and giving her babies what looked like a pretty vigorous bath.

The time was drawing near for me to go back to America, so I found a good home for Mitzi, eight miles from the mission. This was after all her kittens had gotten big enough to give away. Six weeks later she was back again, as lean as a rake and starved nearly to death. I fattened her up and gave her away again. Indeed I gave her away three times before I left Africa. I suppose she came back after we had gone to the coast, for she did not intend to be given away. She wanted to stay where she thought in her feline heart that she belonged, and where she was needed.

Bwantoko

GODFREY CIKOJA was a young man of the Yao tribe in Nyasaland. It is not a highly civilized tribe. Thousands and thousands of them still cling to their old forms and ceremonies of heathen worship, and thousands more of them have embraced the Mohammedan faith.

This tribe of natives was one which was making war on the smaller tribes for the purpose of getting captives to sell into slavery. They had a fixed trade with the Arabs and were enriching themselves on the misery of their fellow Africans.

It is hard to believe that good, kind Godfrey Cikoja belongs to such a wicked people, and that his forefathers were up to such sinful practices. But it is true, and that just goes to show what Christianity can do when it comes into a person's life. It makes fierce people gentle, unkind people kind, hateful people loving. It makes liars tell the truth. There is no power in this world that can take lives and change them as does the power of Christianity.

Godfrey is a big, tall man, and his face is terribly pock-marked, showing that he must have had smallpox earlier in his life. Smallpox is a dreaded disease out there. Whole families, yes, whole villages have been wiped out.

Godfrey lived, when I knew him, in the evangelist's village. Eight small huts had been built, and every two years eight families were brought in, so that there were evangelists in training all the time. The work must be finished in every part of that small country.

Godfrey and his good wife had one sorrow. No children had come to bless their home. Now if Godfrey had not been a Christian, he would have taken another wife; for it was natural that he would have liked little brown babies of his own. But instead of throwing aside his faithful helpmate, he found two little orphan children and gave them love and a home. Again that was a strange thing. The Yaos used to delight in finding orphans, for they could be sold into slavery without any trouble at all—no parents to make trouble. But Godfrey did just the opposite to what his heathen tribe would have done in the days of long ago.

One day Godfrey came up to the mission house to see me. He saw my little native hen come strutting by with her fourteen Rhode Island Red chicks, and his surprise knew no bounds. They were much larger than the baby chicks of his village. Then Hitler, the belligerent old rooster, came swaggering by proudly and watchfully. I warned Godfrey against making any false moves, unless he wanted the fierce rooster to attack him. Instead of inspiring him with fear, Hitler had excited his admiration.

"Ah, crows or the *nyenga* cat will not dare to attack while that fierce soldier is on guard!" he exclaimed. Godfrey had come from a warlike tribe, and he liked the quarrelsome big red rooster.

"I should like very much to have such a fine rooster," he said wistfully. "Then I could begin to build up my flock of chickens, so the hens and the eggs will all be larger."

Then I told him that if he would come over in a few

weeks, after we found out which of the chicks were hens and which were roosters, he would have his rooster. When the little hens had gotten the little shovel-shaped tails, and the little roosters were minus any tail at all, I called Godfrey to come; and he took his little squawking chicken home with him proudly. He told me from time to time that the chicken was growing to be very big indeed.

One day I went on an errand to the evangelist's village. After I got through with my errand, I stopped at the Cikoja house. The little hut was clean and orderly. The pots of grain were piled one on top of the other, so the rats or insects could not get into them to spoil them. An old hen was sitting on some eggs in one corner of the bedroom.

"Oh," cried Godfrey as he saw me. "Have you seen Bwantoko?"

"Bwantoko?" I questioned. "Bwantoko? Why, who is he?"

Then Godfrey laughed delightedly.

"My rooster which you gave to me six months ago," he chuckled. "I named him 'Bwantoko,' for that means 'master' in the Yao language."

Godfrey went over and got a handful of hill rice from one of the pots in the corner. Then he pulled his bamboo chair out in front of the open door.

"Bwantoko! Bwantoko!" he cried.

Suddenly I heard a scurrying rush, and a fine, sleek big rooster came charging across the hard-packed yard, his fine tail feathers fluttering grandly. He streaked into the hut, a guttural gurgle of blabbering joy bubbling out of his wattled neck.

Straight to Godfrey he ran, leaping right onto his knee. He began immediately to eat the rice from Godfrey's cupped palm, audibly voicing his approval and his satisfaction in the finest rooster language.

"Bwantoko, son of Hitler," I thought. Then I got a bright idea. It doesn't matter whose child we are or how lowdown we have been born. No, it does not matter if all of our folks are thieves, robbers, murderers, or jailbirds; we can still be good. We can still have our chance in this world. Anyway, we ought to have as much sense as a rooster and overcome the bad things we inherit from our ancestors.

Henderson's Wife

PASTOR Jonathan Kambambe had a humble pastorate at a place called Msambanjati, which means "the bath place of the buffalo." It is a lucky thing buffaloes do not feel safe enough to come back there to take a bath, for there is no creature in the African bush more dangerous and mean than they. No buffaloes have come there for several years, for too many people live nearby. They do not like people. And people do not like them.

Pastor Jonathan is a humble man, dependable and good. He put a great deal of trust in his oldest son, Henderson, and he wanted him to be a strong man in the work of the Lord. The pastor had little money, but he saw to it that his small son had an education.

When Henderson told his father he had decided to be a teacher, Pastor Jonathan thanked the Lord that He had given him such a wonderful son. He sent Henderson to Malamulo Mission Training School to get his preparation for his lifework. Henderson grew taller and taller until he was almost a foot taller than his humble father.

When Henderson marched into the church on commencement night to get his diploma, old Jonathan whispered to his wife and asked her whether she did not think he was the finest looking one of all the graduates who were marching in. Of course she agreed, and the two of them sat there, happy that their dear son, who was grateful for all they had done for him, was now graduating. Not a week went by that Henderson had not sent them a message of some kind. He seemed to know that his father's and mother's hearts would ache if they were forgotten.

After the graduation Henderson was chosen to go to the northern part of the country to teach. In the place where he had been born, the buffaloes had fled because of the increasing population. Here, there were buffaloes aplenty. A lion or a leopard came only occasionally to Msambanjati, but here they came every night. So Henderson had to be wise and brave too.

Northern Nyasaland is a hard place to live, for the rivers are full of the dreaded crocodiles, and by day the baboons and the monkeys are much thicker. They would destroy all the gardens if a close watch were not kept all the time. And as if that were not enough, wild pigs go forth every night and do a great deal of damage. So the poor black people have a dreadful time, even if the rains do come and the seeds come up. It is a real struggle to live.

Then there is the matter of water. Since most people in civilized countries have water in the kitchen, the bath, the garage, and the yard, it is hard to realize that there are places where water has to be carried for a mile or two for every household need. It is certain that so much water would not be wasted if the people had to lug it around as the people have to do in Africa.

Henderson liked to have clean shirts and trousers when he taught school, so his nice little wife had to wash clothes every day or so. That was because they were poor and did not have many articles of clothing.

Since Mrs. Kambambe did not have any tubs, or a washing machine, or a washboard, she had to take her bundle of clothes down to the river half a mile away to do her washing. Everybody washed clothes that way, and clothing can be gotten sweet and clean when it is washed in clear running water.

One day there had been heavy rains up in the mountains, so the small river was running full and was much deeper and swifter than ordinary. When Henderson saw his young wife pick up her small bundle of clothes and the big, long cake of native soap, he warned her of the deep water.

He was sitting at their small, rough table, making lesson plans as he had been taught to do in training school.

"Be careful," he said. "The rains up in the mountains have been heavy, the people tell me, and the river is deep and swift. You might be carried off your feet."

"I will be careful," she answered shyly.

"Then, again," her husband continued, "crocodiles have been known to enter into small streams when the water is high as it is now. I do not believe there will be any, but keep your eyes open and ask the people you see."

"I will watch," she said again.

"Oh, yes," her husband continued. "Do not take the baby. I will look after him, and that will allow you to come home all the quicker."

The young wife untied the babe and left him with her husband. This one thing saved her life, though she did not realize it at the time.

Soon she was in the middle of the stream, the cool water flowing swiftly around her. She was washing, beating, and resudsing her husband's white shirt. There was a tall, flat clean stone jutting out of the river in the very middle, and this was a favorite place for washing clothes. The clean clothes could be wrung and laid to the back while the other pieces were being washed. She was singing at the top of her voice a song she had learned to sing long ago in Sabbath school. It was, appropriately enough, "Shall We Gather at the River?"

*"Kodi tidzasonkhanadi Pomwe Mtsinjewo wa moyo,
Umayenda nthawi zonse Kwa Mulungummwambamo?"*

Then she launched into the chorus, all the time pounding and beating and pummeling the clothes with all the strength of her smooth brown arms.

*"Inde, tikomane komwe, Ku mtsinje wakukoma wa
    Mulungu;
Tisangane ndi olungama Pa mtsinje mmwambamo."*

To her horror she gazed into the wicked eyes
of a great crocodile that had seized her *nsaru*.

But just here she felt a tug at the *nsaru* cloth she had tied around her. She looked around in great surprise, thinking for a minute it must be some neighbor who had come into the river while she was washing the clothes. But to her horror she gazed into the wicked eyes of a great crocodile that had seized her *nsaru,* which had been floating on the water, and was coming in closer to seize her.

Before she thought, she grabbed the bar of wet soap and hit the creature right across the eyes. Then she made for the shore as fast as the swift current would allow her. She had unfastened the flimsy garment and let him have it while he was battling with the soap in his eyes. She was only a foot or two ahead of the angry beast when she made the bank; but she scrambled up, breathing heavily, and saw it slither back into the water.

She ran all the way back to her husband and her baby, crying all the way. She had been saved! She had been saved! And because she was a Christian, she knew who had saved her.

Her husband came back that evening to see whether he could some way get the clothing his wife had left floating and swishing about on the flat stone. Then he and several of the other men got spears and marched into the water digging in at every step. But the old crocodile must have gone on up the river, for they did not find him.

Henderson brought home all the clothes, even the *nsaru* the crocodile had seized. After the young wife had mended two or three torn places made by the crocodile's ugly teeth, the cloth was as good as ever. But she did not like to wear it very well, for every time she put it on, she remembered ugly eyes and a horrible toothy mouth.

Cosalawa

COSALAWA, son of Kasonga, the former slave, was married to a gentle good wife, who knew how to work and mind her own business. Weja never got into quarrels or fights with the other women in the village. Cosalawa was proud of her and glad she was not like the wife of his brother Amos, who made no end of trouble in the village. He and his wife had a fine little family of boys and girls. They learned to be honest and respectful and how to be still and hold their tongues when it was necessary. Cosalawa sent them all to the mission school, for he did not want them to grow up in ignorance.

As for Cosalawa he had an important position. He had charge of all the foods of the mission. He gave out the meal, the oil, the rice, the beans, the salt, and the sugar to the cook of the boys' compound and to the cook of the girls' compound. Then he gave them peanuts to crush and cook with the wild greens they found in the bush.

In season the boys and girls got tomatoes, onions, pumpkins, papayas, and bananas. Then Cosalawa had charge of the tithe-storage place. Here the people brought the tithe of their gardens and fields; and it was evaluated, paid for, and put with the other mission food supplies.

One day Weja came to him with a strange story. They were sitting by the fire, and the evening meal was over. "The wife of your cousin in the next village was here today," she said quietly.

"Yes?" questioned Cosalawa. He did not like the woman in question, and he did not like to hear that she had come to his house. She was a troublemaker.

"She came about a strange matter," continued the quiet woman, looking sideways at her husband's face. "She began to show me much new cloth she had, a whole basketful. And she had wool, too, a bucketful of it."

Cosalawa turned and looked at his wife in the flickering light of the fire.

"And where did the she-hyena find so many pieces of

One day Weja came to Cosalawa with a strange story.

cloth?" he asked fiercely. "Has she stolen from the Indian store? She is so foolish that she will be caught, and all of us will be cast under suspicion because of her."

"No, Cosalawa," answered Weja. "Yes, it was stolen, but not directly. Down by the stream at the estate is a garden belonging to the *bwana*. She often goes there in the night-time and takes a few things, and then the next day she goes to some Europeans and sells them. She says she has found several good gardens, and she takes a little something every night.

Cosalawa jumped to his feet. "What kind of cousin do I have, to be led by such a hyena?" he shouted. "She will pull him and his whole family into the mud, for she will be caught. You know she will, and she will be beaten for being a thief."

"And that is not all, Cosalawa," his wife continued softly. "She told me that I, too, could have cloth and wool and sugar and teacups if I went and took just a little from your storehouse every day."

Cosalawa turned upon her fiercely, but when he saw the look in her eyes, the anger died within him.

"And what did you say to that hyena, Weja, my wife?" he asked, marveling at her calm and her sweetness.

"I told her," answered Weja quietly, "that no cloth, no wool, no teacups, were worth selling the honor of Cosalawa. It was not worth it for his sons and his daughters to see that the father is not a man but a lizard who can run here and there but to no purpose. I told her I wanted my sons to grow up in the shadow of the honor of the family, the true sons of Cosalawa and Kasonga. I told her to go away from my house and never to come back until she came back with honor."

"*Mkazi wabwino,*" murmured Cosalawa. He knew his

wife was a good woman. And he was not afraid to tell her so.

Around the fire that night, listening to his conversation, were the sons of Cosalawa. The oldest was Leckion. He learned to love honesty and truth at the humble home of his father and mother. He learned it by listening to the small conversations, to the ideals and beliefs of a humble man and a humble woman.

When I went to Africa, Leckion Cosalawa was my first houseboy. Before he came to my house to take the job, Cosalawa called the young man to him.

"Remember," he said, "you are the son of Cosalawa, an honest man. You are the grandson of Kasonga, who worshiped God before he ever knew His name. He was a man of great honor and truth. See that you remember well the records of those before you, and keep your character clean."

He did. I could trust everything to his care. He was a faithful steward of all my goods.

Leckion, Son of Cosalawa

AS SOON as I looked into the strong face of Leckion, I knew that I could trust him. I simply knew it. As time went on, I realized more and more how fine it is to have someone in charge of your house and your things who is absolutely trustworthy. At that time I had a cook boy in the kitchen whom I was not so sure about. He had shifty eyes, a loud, blustering manner, and was filled with egotism and braggadocio. His name was Iail. He spent a great deal of time ordering Waison, his helper, about in a high-handed manner and doing nothing that I could see. Then I began to notice that I was buying more groceries than I had ever bought in all my married life. We never sweetened cereals or hot drinks, yet the sugar disappeared in wholesale lots, and no one seemed to know why the tin was always empty. Five pounds would walk out in two days. I had not used five pounds in a month before.

Raisins, plums, prunes, and peas simply were not there when I went to get them. The way butter and cream disappeared you would have thought we bathed in the cream and waxed our floors, washed our hair, and oiled all the mission machinery with the butter.

Then the papayas and the mangoes never seemed to get

ripe for me. I'd see one almost ready to eat, but when I spoke of it, Iail would say hurriedly, "No, no, this is not the time for ripening, madam." He was fattening up on my ignorance. And I was learning fast.

I noticed that Leckion became thoughtful. He would start to say something; then he would close his mouth quickly as if he were awaiting a more auspicious time. He wanted to tell me something, but he did not know how to do it.

Then Iail, in a hatefully confidential way, told me one day to get rid of Leckion. He would get me a fine houseboy, one I would like ever so much better than I did that slow donkey.

"No, Iail. I like Leckion, and I will not get rid of him. I am sure of him. He is a fine young man. I have no reason to get rid of him."

But Iail did not give up easily. He stood his ground and leaned toward me. "But he is a thief, madam. Your things are not safe in his hands."

I looked Iail straight in the eyes. He could not stand the straight scrutiny and dropped his eyes instantly.

"Iail, you know that is not so. It is not Leckion who is the thief. There is a thief; of that I am sure, but it is not Leckion."

I saw a kind of terror in Iail's eyes as he turned to go away. For a moment I felt like telling him to go then and there, but somehow I did not. I did not know that Leckion heard the whole of the conversation, for he was in the small bathroom scrubbing the tin tub at the time. He emerged presently, a quiet smile on his strong face—so much like the face of Cosalawa, his father.

For several days Iail was scrupulous in taking care of things in the kitchen. He was nervous and offered a solution to the disappearances every time I went into the kitchen. But he did not have a change of heart, so when I began to teach, things began to get bad again. He would not resist the delicacies that were mine.

We were getting ready to move into the bigger mission house recently vacated by a mission family who went home on permanent return. Leckion went up and scrubbed every floor, waxed and polished them, and I got my things packed for the move. Iail was supposed to pack the kitchen things, but when I went into the kitchen, he was gone.

"Where did Iail go?" I asked Waison. He looked scared. I got curious. "Waison," I said, "is Iail bad to you?"

Waison looked more scared than ever. He looked to the right hand and to the left. He could not speak English well, and I was new in the country. I could not speak Cinyanja, the native tongue, at all.

"Iail . . . he very bad man," he stammered in a low, scared voice. "He steal . . . he beat me . . . he tell me . . . not tell."

"Thank you, Waison," I said. "I know this, and I will not let him hurt you. He cannot be my cook boy."

"You chase him?" he whispered. "He not beat me?"

"Yes, I will chase [discharge] him," I promised. "I will chase him today." The day before, after Leckion and I had worked in the new house a long time, I walked through to look it over. The furniture was crude. The mattresses were homemade. There was a big bowl and pitcher set on a washstand in the bedroom. In fact there was one in every bedroom. I noted one in particular. It was a bright blue and had a red rose on the side as big as a cabbage. I laughed a little at the garish decoration, but I was thankful for the antique sets in the absence of plumbing.

After my conversation with Waison, Leckion and I set

out toward the other house, which was at the top of the mission hill. We were walking along, Leckion keeping a little in the background as a mark of respect. Just then I saw Iail emerge from the new house. What in the world was *he* doing up there? I had not sent him. Surely he had been up to no good. He should have been in the kitchen packing as I had told him to do.

Iail did not recognize Leckion and me at first until he was halfway down the hill on his bicycle. Steep as the hill is, he stopped and looked at us coming as if he were not at all eager to meet us. Then on a sudden impulse, he got off his bicycle and started to wheel it off into the bush. I knew then for sure he had been up to mischief, for there was no bush path there and no reason for him to leave the road. But he seemed bent on escaping.

He went on down the hill, and I stood looking after him, undecided what to do.

Then I yelled like a fishwife to the disappearing Iail.

"Iail," I bellowed. I heard Leckion laughing softly behind me.

Most reluctantly, and very, very slowly, Iail came back into the path. He dared not ignore me, and he hardly moved. He did not raise his eyes as we drew near.

"Where have you been, Iail?" I asked.

"I went to the new house to see if there was pussly in the garden," he mumbled.

"Parsley?" I questioned. "That was a silly thing for you to do. We have more parsley at the old house than we can eat in a hundred years," I said. "Anyway I told you to pack, not to hunt parsley."

Then I let my eyes drop to his bicycle. I gasped. There, tied to his bicycle, was part of my washstand set, the one with the large red roses on a bright blue background. Surely that was it, surely there had not been others he could buy at markets or get someplace legitimately. I decided not to accuse him until I checked, for I have a horror of false accusations.

"I wanted fine pussly for the madam," murmured Iail lamely.

He went on down the hill, and I stood looking after him, undecided what to do. "Isn't that part of the china bedroom set there from the guest room?" I asked Leckion. "You washed it yesterday."

"It is a part of it," he said simply. "Iail, he has taken it. He did not have any parsley."

As soon as we went to the house, I went immediately and checked the bowl set. Yes, one piece was missing. Iail had sneaked in and had taken it. If I had not met him, I would never have known where it was gone.

I turned to Leckion, who was watching me closely.

"Go down and get what Iail stole," I said quietly. "And tell Iail I want to see him. He cannot work for me any more. Nothing is safe when he is around. I cannot have a thief in my house."

Then Leckion spoke.

"When I came to work for you, Cosalawa, my father, told me, 'Take nothing from the house of the Dona. No, not even a pin or a small needle. If you think the madam has thrown something away, ask her. If she wants you to have it, she will give it to you."

"Yes, Leckion," I answered, "you have been faithful and honorable. I knew I could trust you."

"Well, I heard the words of Iail against my character one day. I was washing the bath when he came to tell you to watch out for me since he knew me to be a thief."

"Do you know, Leckion," I answered, "I think he wanted you out of the house so he need not be so careful as to what he stole from me. He wanted to get another one just like himself in the house."

"I have some words to tell you about Bee's Moss, the wood boy," continued Leckion. "Iail is the one who found him, and he is the one who carries away the things Iail takes away from your kitchen. He has often been in jail for his stealing. Do not ever buy the bananas from him. He always steals them."

"I will get a new wood and water boy," I said. Later on I got one who was the deacon in the Kaipsya village church, and he worked for me until the day I left Malamulo and sailed for America.

Leckion worked for me until I urged him to go farther in school so he could get a job more fitted to his high intelligence. He first went to a place where he learned to be a tailor. In this way he made his own shirts and trousers and those of Cosalawa. Then he was eager to learn more, so he learned typing and bookkeeping. He is now the secretary and confidential clerk for a great chief. He has a very good job indeed. It is a job of high honor, for the chief, his master, is a strong one and well known. But Leckion serves still a higher Chief, even Jesus, as does Cosalawa and as did Kasonga.

Bee's Moss has been in and out of jail again and again. Iail hated to leave my work, but he saw he was caught at his slippery game. He came with his book and tried to get me to recommend him. I told him I could not do so, for I did not think he was a good cook boy for me. He had many different jobs, but none of them lasted long, because he could not keep his hands off other people's belongings.

Isaac John

BETWEEN the new school building and the old post office building, a pathway meanders down the hill toward the Nambichamba River at old Malamulo Mission. That path is venerated by the memory of an old, old chieftain who used to live nearby. Before he died, he liked to come over to Malamulo and tell the people of the greatest event in his life. He usually stood there and looked down the hill, a dreamy look in his old eyes.

"Right here it was . . . right here. I saw the greatest man who ever lived—David Livingstone. He slept in a small tent right where those trees bend over, and he was making ready to go when I came that morning to pay my respects and to bring him a fowl and some eggs. I can see him, as if it were yesterday, going down that path. Just as he got by the river, he turned and waved at us.

" 'Tsalani bwino,' was what he said there, telling us good-by in our own language. Oh, we could not help but love him, for we could all see he was here to help us."

Down that same little path, which has been worn by the footfalls of man and beast, people still travel every day. The Malamulo Dairy is on the banks of the river, making it possible for the equipment to be washed in plenty of clean, clear water. Over a rickety bridge the milk boys come every morning and evening with their petrol tins of frothy milk, treading blithely over the structure, so rickety that one wonders why it has not fallen down long before this.

Across the stream the path winds again, around and around, until the big dip tanks are in view. Here the cattle are driven every week, whether they like it or not, and are forced to go through the water, which has a strong antitick and anti-insect repellent dissolved in it. They bawl and fight it, poor, foolish things, but how wretched they would be without it! They can go back to the kraals in comparative comfort for another week.

When the pathway at last achieves the top of the hill, the buildings are fairly close together, almost elbowing one another. Four primitive barns with homemade stanchions are at the left. Just ahead are several huge silage pits where the cattle feed is chopped and put for fermentation against the weeks when the pastures are dry and sparse. At the right is a long line of houses, the first one in the row being the home of Isaac John, the chief cattle herder. Right near to this humble little mud hut is a rocky hill. Another structure peeps over the high boulders at the top. What is it? A small beaten path leads to the top. It will be easy to find out.

Only poles, bamboo, and mud . . . with a grass roof. Yet this is different. There are pews here. Rough, yes, but pews. This is a church. It is almost as primitive, clean, and windswept as the groves which were God's first temples. One sinks down on the rough log, which is a pew, and asks the Lord to bless him in this holy place; for holy it is and sanctified to the worship of the Lord. The mud floor has been freshly mudded and smoothed by loving hands until it almost shines. There is a rough pulpit, made by Isaac John's brown hands, and a place where he can lay his Holy Bible.

There is a small village nearby, which the mission people call Gibeah because the heathen live there. Most of the cattle herders of Isaac John are raw heathen, and he would have it so. He hungers and thirsts after souls. His heavy duties and responsibilities with the cattle herd are not enough for this good man. Every evening, after the milking is done, Isaac John's herders meet in the little chapel up in the rocks. The head herdsman has had perhaps one grade of education. The only book he can read well is the Bible. The only thing he can write well is his own name. Other words are poorly spelled and so poorly scrawled as to be almost unreadable. But he can sing and preach and pray with the eloquence of an apostle. He can and does lead people to the kingdom of God.

He teaches them to sing:

"Ambuye ali pafudi kudza
Ndikumva concodi
Ndipo nyenyenze zikuzima
Tsopano ndi mbanda kucatu."

They can hardly wait to ask him, "Why, Isaac John, this song says it's almost time for the Lord to come. Who is this Lord? Why is He coming? Where is He coming from? And why should this concern us?"

Then is Isaac John's chance. This is just what he wants. A smile comes over his good face as he tells his heathen listeners the story of the love of Jesus, our blessed Saviour. He tells them of His good life spent healing and teaching the people. He tells them of the cruel cross, the garden tomb. He tells them the glorious news that the grave, that death, could not hold the Son of God, for He arose as He said He would on the third day and is now in heaven where He is preparing a place for those who love Him.

"And, oh, my brothers!" cries Isaac John with an eloquence which touches the hearts of those who are listening, "such a wondrous place He has gone to prepare for us . . . for you and for me . . . not just for the white people. We shall all sit down together in that good land. He has made houses for all His children. He has built a house for me. Not of straw, or mud, or brick, or kimberly blocks. Oh, no, we will live in houses of silver and of gold. And we will never find any lack of water. The gardens will always be growing. There will be no cold . . . no malaria . . . no wild beasts."

"No famines? No hunger?" cry several incredulous voices. "How can this be? Where is this country?"

Then into this small, rough bush chapel creeps the indescribable presence of the Lord. Isaac John, who had but little schooling, is well versed in matters of the kingdom of God. One wonders how he, who had never had a comfort or a luxury in all his life, could know so much about the land that is fairer than day.

One morning, very early, he was hurrying up the mission road so fast that it seemed as if the appointment he must make was urgent indeed. He met one of the missionaries.

"Where are you going so early, Isaac John?" she asked. "You have probably been up since two or three this morning with the milkers. You must be tired."

He smiled his shy, humble smile. "I am going to a village over by Cholo Mountain."

"But that is far, Isaac John. It must be eight or ten miles across the bush."

"It is, madam. And I must hurry. The boys came late for the milking this morning, and that makes me late. You see," he smiled again, "I preach there every day. The people are waiting for me."

He was hurrying up the mission road so fast that it seemed as if the appointment he must make was urgent indeed.

And he was off down the road, his ragged clothes fluttering and his horny, bare feet barely skimming the road, so fast did he go.

One Sabbath day he brought a chief, pompous and important in his robes and regalia, to the church. He was one of those who had been attending his early morning meetings, and this was his first Sabbath to attend church.

When baptism time comes at Malamulo, Isaac John is an interested observer. He can see those for whom he has labored come up out of the water to walk in "newness of life." He has won scores of the heathen people to Christianity. Many will walk the streets of gold because a simple cow herder glorified his menial job.

The world might say that Isaac John is just a poor, ignorant native. But he isn't. Not at all. For the Book of God plainly says, "He that winneth souls is wise."

Wisdom Is Humble

THERE is an old proverb that says, "A little knowledge is a dangerous thing." There are some people who think they are the smartest people in the world if they have just a small amount of education. They speak with great authority out of the great abundance of their ignorance.

And there are others who have had a fine chance in life but who are so proud and exalted and lifted up that you can't touch them with a ten-foot pole. Neither one of these classes does a great deal of good in this world.

Great scientists like George Washington Carver, who have had a small glimpse into the grandeur and the glory of the undiscovered marvels, exhibited great humility. The story is told that Dr. Carver once asked the Lord, "Lord, why did you make this world?" The Lord replied, "My child, you could not understand if I told you." "Then, Lord, why did you make me?" the young man persisted. "That, too, my boy is beyond your comprehension." After a while he asked again, "Lord, why did you make the peanut?" "Now that, my son, I can tell you. But it will take much study and years of hard work for you to know even a small part of it."

But Kuya was bitten by the bug that he was SOME-BODY. Even the way he walked, the way he swaggered around, showed that he thought he was the most important young man for miles around the mission. Of course he was not a favorite. People did not like him very well, but he thought proudly that it was because they were too ignorant to appreciate him. He did not pity the poor, ignorant people around him, but he often sneered at them, even laughed at their blunders and mistakes. All this pride had come upon him like a flood, because he had successfully passed a higher grade than some of his African brothers. He had reached the equivalent of the ninth or the tenth grade.

Not many of the poor ones in Africa have the chance to go that far in school. Indeed there are tens of thousands who never see the inside of a schoolroom, for there are not nearly enough facilities that even a large fraction of the people have the privilege of a little schooling. Kuya, instead of feeling humbly grateful that the Lord had blessed him so abundantly, was all puffed up and proud, as the Bible said the scribes and the Pharisees were when Jesus walked on earth.

Satan keeps on working with a person who yields himself to his wicked deceit and lying sophistries. After a while Kuya began to feel himself superior to the godly teachers on the mission, the mission which specialized in keeping all the commandments of God. He began to think it was not to his advantage to be so peculiar. He began to strut around like a banty rooster on stilts. If it had not been so sad, it would have been funny; for even David exclaimed long, long ago to God, "What is man, that thou art mindful of him?"

Early one morning Kuya ran away. He had gotten it into his head that he was very, very desirable and that whoever got him as a teacher was lucky indeed. He went at a foolish time. His class was reviewing for the government examinations which were to be written in about eight weeks. When the news came as to where he went, it was found that Kuya had gone to offer his valuable services to the Nyasaland government, fully expecting to take his examinations in the government offices by special favor, as he thought fitted his exalted position.

But Kuya got his first jolt. Her Majesty's officer of education was hardly civil to him and bade him to be gone in no uncertain terms. He crept out of there, dazed and indecisive as to what to do. It was all unexpected. He could hardly believe his ears. But he was not deflated, not yet. It would take more than that to knock the wind out of him, for his self-adulation was chronic by this time.

Then he thought of the great Church of Scotland Mission Training School some five or six hundred miles to the north. Kuya's sense of superiority revived. He used all the money he and all his relatives had to get up there. He went by truck, cart, foot, or any way he could find. He played everything on this one chance.

Ah! There they would appreciate him! They would be able to see at a glance what a valuable teacher he would be! Even though he was footsore and tired almost to exhaustion when he arrived, so confident was he that he applied for an interview with the headmaster immediately.

The shrewd Scot who headed up this fine school listened quietly to Kuya's long-spun story that had the words "I," "me," "my," and "mine" far too often. The older man seemed bored and impatient. He tapped the desk with his fingers. He was canny and a wise judge of human nature. Suddenly he interrupted the long, tiresome, repetitious tale.

"And why," he asked quietly, "*why* did you leave the mission where you got your training? Surely if you are the paragon you say you are, you owe your training to some

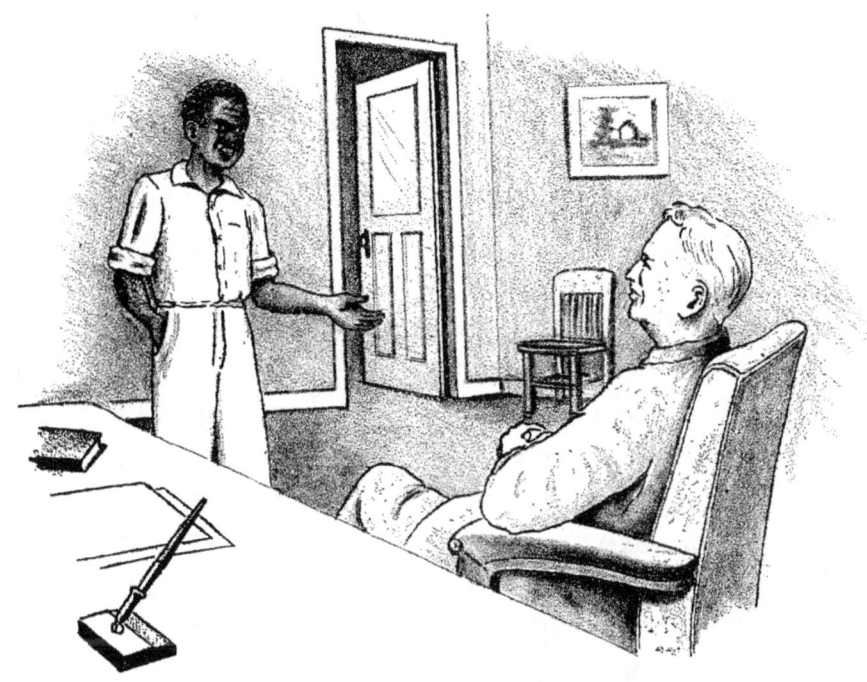

"Well," Kuya stammered, "I do not think
they really appreciated my capabilities."

good school. Surely you were not born with all these
virtues."

"Well," Kuya stammered, "I do not think they really
appreciated my abilities. They often reprimanded me and
corrected me."

"I do not think, my boy, that your school owes you any
appreciation. But *you* owe your school a lot of it. You
have selfishly taken benefits from your mission and your
school for several years. Now the time has almost come
that you can, in a small way, repay the debt you owe and
that you ought to be glad to pay. But, no. You come here
babbling foolishness about your not being appreciated. You
want to run out on a just obligation. No, my boy, we cannot
admit you to our school. I love loyalty."

Kuya stood looking at the old educator with unbelief in his eyes. Then the cold finger of fear touched his heart. Had he heard aright? Was there something wrong with his eyes and his ears?

"Were your teachers mean to you? Did they starve you, kick you, cheat you, beat you?" The burning, hostile eyes of the good old man were on Kuya's face.

"Oh, no, sir. I have no complaints along that score."

"Then what are you complaining of? And why did you come here? We do not owe you anything. You do not owe us anything. We have never done a thing for you, and I am glad we did not. You would have been wanting to run out on us, I take it, as you are doing your own mission."

"B-b-but, sir, isn't there an opening for me here?"

"Yes, there is," snapped the old man, tired of the interruption and the waste of time. He pointed to the door.

"There is your opening. And see that you close it when you go out. Go back to your mission, if they will have you, which I doubt, and thank God, if they do, that you have been given the chance to repay some of your benefits."

Kuya found himself outside—chagrin, shame, and astonishment filling his whole head and heart. He was nearly wild with worry. He had only one place he could go now, and he had almost burned the bridges back. That was to the mission which had benefited him and given him all he had—to the mission he had despised and spurned. He had no money to ride, and he had nearly five hundred miles to walk, and only a mere three weeks until the time for examinations. What could he eat on the road? Where would he stay without pennies to pay for a place to lay his blanket? Would they take him if he did get back?

But he started that very day to walk back. He had so little to eat and endured so many hardships and privations that he was a bag of bones when he got to the mission, a mere caricature of his sleek, arrogant self. His feet were so blistered and lacerated that he had them wrapped in old rags when he limped up to his teacher's house.

His kind Christian teacher could see in a minute that he had suffered horribly in his small self-staged rebellion, so he was allowed to plead his case—not with pride, but now with abject humility and self-recriminations. After a long discussion, under which he suffered keenly from suspense and fear, Kuya was told that he would be allowed to take his examinations. His lesson in humility was well learned, for Kuya is now a fine teacher, faithful and loyal for the mission which gave him all that he has.

We Go on Our Coastal Furlough

WHEN my husband and I first arrived at Malamulo four years ago, we scoffed at the idea that we would need a mid-term furlough. Fortunately we did not have the say-so. Older and more seasoned missionaries know that three and a half years of a hot equatorial climate is enough at a stretch for persons born and reared in a temperate zone.

School was out in August, so we began to fill the big packing boxes once again. What should we take? As little as possible. We wanted to save as much room as we could to bring things back from "civilization." Down came the pictures. Up came the rugs. Dishes were wrapped. Drawers were emptied. Books were sorted and packed away. My husband nailed up the boxes as fast as I packed them.

My tomatoes were ripening, and since the famine had pinched so long, I did not want to pack one empty fruit jar. Good old black Cook Batison in my kitchen canned tomatoes, tomatoes, and tomatoes. Lester, the pot washer and general errand boy, rushed here and there doing a whole multitude of things. Alice, our standard-eight native girl, who helps me with sewing, knitting, and mending, seemed to be everywhere at once. Francis, the standard-seven boy who takes care of the yard and garden, washed clothes, ironed, wiped up floors, and mourned over the fact that we were not going to be able to eat the pineapples, oranges, and papayas which would ripen in abundance after we were gone.

At last the great day came. Our car was all loaded, ready to go. The boys who work for us stood in a disconsolate row, tears slipping down their black faces. Daddy Lee, my husband's stepfather, my husband, and I sat in the front seat. Alice sat in the back with some of our luggage that we could not get into the trunk. She went with us to help me with my work while I tried to recover, for the tropics had not been kind to me. Perhaps if I had rest and relaxation, the cool, salty air would make me feel well again.

We looked back once at our rambling mission house. The grass around it was burned to an ugly, sear brown. The hedge looked sick and pallid. My porch plants had died long ago of the drought. The sun beat mercilessly down upon us as we drove carefully around the curves of the narrow bush road. Our long journey was begun. It was high noon, Wednesday, September 28, 1949.

Mile after mile, hour after hour, we journeyed on. Our first destination was Matandani Mission. Pastor and Mrs. O. I. Fields had invited us to spend our first night on the way out with them.

Darkness was falling when we stopped in front of the big, homey mission house. The rooms were large and airy and looked inviting and comfortable. The table was set when we went in, and the food looked and smelled delicious.

The next morning we started out early, for we had the hot Zambezi Valley to traverse. Everyone warned us that we would be scorched! Mrs. Fields saw to it that our lunch kit was well stocked. All three thermos bottles were filled with ice water. The two tin sandwich boxes held delicious hard-boiled egg sandwiches, and there was one box of ripe tomatoes.

After a little time we crossed the customs barrier and were permitted to enter Portuguese East Africa, or Mozambique. It was a most dreary country, for rain had not fallen for months, and the streams were dry. Dust lay deep on the miserable roads, and ant hills high as houses flourished in boulder-strewn fields. The animals, what few we saw, were lean and ill favored. Hour after hour all we saw was burned grass, sand, rocks, and ant hills. When we passed villages, the people seemed poor and dispirited. Their houses were tumbled down and dilapidated and surrounded by refuse and broken pottery. Thin, scrawny chickens pecked hungrily all around the doors, and thin Kaffir dogs snarled and slunk away.

The wind coming through the open car windows was scorching; but at last, when we thought we could bear it no longer, we turned an abrupt corner, and there lay the Zambezi River in full view. There was no shade, so we stopped as near the place where the ferry came in as possible.

We got out our little lunch box and ate dinner there on the banks of the Zambezi. Alice and I took our dishes down to the river to wash them. Our feet burned, so we took off our shoes and stockings and waded after our dishes were washed and dried. Daddy Lee and my husband saw the fun we were having, and they came and joined us. We stayed inside a small cove behind a couple of fishing boats, for we were in no mood to furnish a lunch to some hungry crocodile. The ferry came at last, and we soon found ourselves in Tete, a Portuguese town on the other side of the river.

All three of our thermos bottles were empty by this time,

so we set about trying to fill them. If we had wanted to get them filled with beer or gin, we would have had no trouble whatsoever; but water was quite a different matter. At last we found an Asiatic Indian who led us into a beautiful patio full of potted plants and blooming trees. There hanging in a tree was a waterpot, which contained surprisingly cool water. We drank and drank and filled our bottles and went on our way.

The country continued desolate, sandy, and dreary to the extreme.

The next morning dawned hot and clear. We ate hastily so we could be first to cross the customs barriers into Southern Rhodesia. Friday morning! Preparation day—where would we spend the Sabbath?

After a little while we came into a prettier country. Green fields stretched down to rocky little streams, and sometimes cows stood knee deep in the clear water. A great nostalgia swept over me. Could this be Africa? It seemed more like Iowa. At last we came into the clean city of Salisbury, Southern Rhodesia, the first real town I had seen for four years. I took Alice into the bright, gaily decked stores so like our own in the United States. Her mother had died in Johannesburg when she was only six, so she could not remember much except mud huts, bush roads, and tumbledown primitive Indian stores in the villages clustering about Lake Nyasa.

The escalators especially took her childlike fancy. Every time I missed her, I would go and look for the moving stairways, and there I would see her brown face covered with smiles as she rode up and down, up and down, ecstatically. When I attempted to cross the street with the stop light, I had to hold tightly to her, for she was not sure at all that the string of motorcars would not start up suddenly and run us down. I explained to her that they must not go until the light turned green, so she calmed down a bit, but she still was on constant guard.

My good husband bought me the first ice-cream cone I had had in four years. I bought a bottle of olives and a loaf of raisin bread. I found a box of soda crackers, such as we had not tasted for years. It was like manna in the wilderness. It was delightful to walk past shop windows and look at things—at bright towels, flowered lunch cloths, and pretty drinking glasses. We looked and looked and looked. We had to tear ourselves away, for we well knew that it was Friday, and we needed to find a place to get ready for Sabbath and to sleep that night. We headed toward Fort Victoria. About the middle of the afternoon my husband spied a house which was set far back from the road.

"These people probably have water," he said. "Maybe they will let us camp near their house."

So Daddy Lee opened the big gate, and we drove down a winding road to the house. We got out to investigate but found it empty, deserted. However, the dooryard was clean, and we found water and a place to set up camp.

While the men got other things ready, Alice and I prepared supper. I had found canned soup in Salisbury. Soup, crackers, potatoes boiled in their jackets, raisin bread and butter, topped with cling peaches made a supper fit for a king. We separated then with a bar of soap, towel, and pan of water apiece, and behind convenient bushes or shrubs we all had a bath and were ready for the Sabbath. It was more fun than bathing in a tiled tub in some uninteresting civilized place. Then Alice built up a big fire, and we pulled out our cushions and sat around it. My husband read from his Bible, and we had a most beautiful time of worship there under the stars.

Alice built up a big fire, and we pulled
out our cushions and sat around it.

"Lord, thou hast been our dwelling place in all generations. Before the mountains were brought forth, or ever thou hadst formed the earth and the world, even from everlasting to everlasting, thou art God." "And let the beauty of the Lord our God be upon us: and establish thou the work of our hands upon us; yea, the work of our hands establish thou it."

And that was indeed our prayer. Our hearts were sore on leaving our dear black children for six long months; we well knew that our work had been human and feeble and at times faulty. If God would indeed bless the work of our hands, as He had promised, and make it grow to be mighty in Christ Jesus, how happy we would be!

Then we blew up our mattresses, got out our blankets, and went to sleep.

14

The next day, at the Fort Victoria church, my husband met a cousin of his, secretary-treasurer of the Southern African Division many years ago, Otho Fortner. How glad we were for a visit with him! It was a beautiful Sabbath day, and at sundown we reluctantly said good-by and headed south. We had heard that there was a delightful rest camp near the world-famous Zimbabwe ruins.

Sure enough, a long row of rondawels had been prepared for travelers. Night had fallen when we rented one that was erected on a great flat stone. Behind it a grill had been built for cooking food, and near at hand was a tank to which water was hauled by oxcart every day. Naturally we had to boil every drop of our drinking water.

The next day we went out to look over the ruins. When was Zimbabwe built? By whom? Certainly until this riddle is answered, a great gap must remain in the history of this mysterious continent.

For many generations these mysterious ruins in Mashonaland have been the subject of bitter controversy among archaeologists. Even today no one solution is generally accepted. As many theories as I have fingers and toes have been advanced to explain how Zimbabwe came into being, and by whom it was built. Some suggest that this ancient gold field was the destination of Phoenicians, sent by King Solomon, according to Hebrew records, to bring gold and some other products from distant lands.

Many maintain that the Ophir spoken of in the Bible was really the modern port of Sofala, and that Havilah was none other than Mashonaland. Be that as it may, there certainly was once at Zimbabwe a civilization which produced architecture that rivals anything we have seen in present native architecture.

One of the most imposing ruins of the many to be seen

is the temple fortress, elliptical in shape, with a stone floor, and with walls of great height and thickness. The bricks, hand hewn of stone, are laid together to fit without mortar, as were the stones of Solomon's Temple. What slaves of long, long ago hewed these millions of bricks? Under whose lash did tens of thousands of miserable men erect these mighty structures? Certainly their religion must have been similar to that of Babylon.

We could not miss the acropolis, a fortified hill, over two hundred feet in height. We climbed up the ancient ascent laid by patient hands nobody knows how many centuries ago. Yet the steps are still good, winding in and out and up, worn by numberless bare feet through the centuries. It took a long time to climb to the top of the tortuous path, which suddenly grows alarmingly precipitous, and made us scramble with care over stones slippery with moss. Then suddenly we were before the gates of the great fortress.

We crept through the small passageway in the walls twelve feet thick and came into the ruinous grandeur of a mighty audience chamber. Then we went through an array of long corridors, other audience chambers, smelting rooms, and overhead bridges. The stonework was surprisingly smooth and even. What strange peoples once lived here? We could only guess as have others wiser than we.

After we had returned to the camp, Alice and I decided to do some washing. I hunted out all our soiled clothes while she scrubbed a clean place on the boulder by the water tank. Then she got down on her knees, and so deftly soaped and beat, soaped and beat, that the dirty water ran in every direction. I tried to imitate her, but was not a success. So I went and found some trees near together and put up a little clothesline.

The next day we entered Kruger Park, a wild animal

preserve probably two hundred miles in length. Here wild beasts are left free to roam, eat, breed, and stalk their prey, as they did before the white man penetrated Africa. It is perhaps the largest wild-animal sanctuary in all the world.

We got our booklets, directions, and warnings at Punda Maria. We must not carry firearms. We must never take any risk in regard to elephants. If they showed fight or anger, we must get away, and get away fast. We were told of one elephant who in a playful mood sat down on the hood of a car. The car folded up like an accordion. By the time we reached Shingwedzi, the next camp, we were ever so excited, and chattered about all the wild things we had seen. One elephant evinced a faint interest in our welfare, flapped his giant caladium-shaped ears, and gestured at us with his wormlike trunk. We did not stop, even though he seemed to be inviting us to have tea with him.

We went right on and set up camp in a whitewashed hut. There we had fun cooking eggs in my aluminum folding skillet, warming up soup, and toasting bread over the open fire at the grill. Our hut was equipped with three beds boasting innerspring mattresses. In the night we could hear the cries of the wild beasts outside our enclosure.

The last night we spent in the wild animal run was in a tent in the Skikuza Camp. The sky was overcast, and it looked as though it might rain any minute. But the storm held off till we were in bed, and then it began to *pour*. The tent leaked like a sieve. But we got through the night with no other ill effects than dampened ardor and blankets, and we went on our way rejoicing. We had materially added to our list of wild animals even though we had not seen any lions. Once several large giraffes galloped along in front of the car.

We had hardly started that morning before we came upon

two big lions, a male and a female, lapping water from a puddle in the middle of the road. Off to the left another lioness came sauntering out of the bush and smelled all around our car. We had rolled up our windows hastily, not wishing to accommodate any feline hitch-hikers. The big lioness looked amiable and placid, as if she might purr if I got out and stroked her, but I did not do so. Appearances sometimes are deceiving. Finally she lay down beside the car and indulged in a good nap.

Then the two lions in front of us finished drinking and came over to the car. The male was in the lead, his mouth open, and water dripping from his great teeth and chops. I heard a muffled sound behind me and saw Alice trying to ascend the pile of luggage on the back seat.

We had to laugh even as we assured her that if the beasts did not get the man smell, we would be all right and safe in the car. Lions are no joke to Africans. Alice knows people who have been attacked and killed by these great cats of the bush. The text that tells us that Satan is going about as a roaring lion is tremendously real to them. They know only too well how menacing and deadly our adversary is.

It was Friday again! We were near to the asbestos- and gold-mining town of Barberton in the Transvaal. Alice had told us that she had a cousin living there who had been very near to her dear mother. She was a nurse in the hospital at Barberton.

First, we found the rest camp the city maintained for travelers. It was built rondawel style in green terraces up the side of a beautiful mountain. Our cabin was neat and clean, equipped with table, chairs, comfortable beds, and a clothes rack. Cretonne curtains were looped back from the windows.

A neat laundry house with bathrooms was just a step

away. Here a great stove was kept roaring hot to heat water for baths and for cooking.

We unloaded the car, made the beds, and got settled for the Sabbath. Then we went over to the hospital to look up Alice's cousin. We found her in charge of one section of the native unit. This woman had given Alice her name at birth, but had not seen her since her mother had died fifteen years before. Her father in his helplessness and grief had taken his little children off to his own heathen tribe and family, up on the banks of Lake Nyasa. Then he too had sickened and died. It seemed as if the bush had swallowed them completely.

I walked into the place and inquired for the cousin.

"Where is Miriam Nkosi?"

I heard a muffled cry beside me, and a tall, fine-looking African nurse in a crisp, white uniform stood before me.

"I am Miriam Nkosi, madam," she said simply.

"I have brought you your cousin, Alice Princess Msumba."

For a moment Miriam looked dazed. Then when the words I had said seemed to sink into her understanding, she ran up to Alice, swept her into her great motherly arms, and showered her brown face with kisses.

"Akim and Lena's little girl!" she cried with wonder.

Then almost shamefacedly she apologized to me.

"You must pardon me, madam," she cried, the tears standing in her eyes. "This is a thing I have hoped for and prayed for, but never thought that God would grant to me. I have prayed and prayed for this hour."

How those loving arms felt to Alice I could only guess. Her kind mother and father were only dim memories. Her home life was so far in the past that it seemed only a beautiful dream. She could but dimly remember her mother in their home near the City Deep Hospital in Johannesburg. Then came the dreary interim with the father's backward tribe up on the banks of Lake Nyasa. What wonder that Miriam's clean, kind face, representative of her mother's people, seemed like that of an angel to gentle Alice!

Miriam invited us to come to her house that evening and promised that the Methodist church choir to which she belonged would sing for us in Zulu and in English. For two hours we sat and listened to the native choirmaster and the pastor lead their group in lovely music so full of clicks and imitable sounds peculiar to the Xosa and Zulu tongues.

Then they closed with a most lovely song, so full of wailing and longing, so full of unanswered yearning, that our hearts were touched.

> "Give a thought to Africa
> Beneath the burning sun.
> There are hosts of weary hearts
> Waiting to be won.
> Many lives have passed away,
> But on land and sea
> There are voices crying now
> For the living God.
> Tell the love of Jesus
> By her hills and waters.
> God bless Africa
> And her sons and daughters."

The next day was Sabbath. By inquiry we found that there was a church which met at the schoolhouse in the Asiatic Indian location. Sabbath school had just begun when we found the place and entered. A fine young Indian superintendent acknowledged our presence courteously and in prayer asked God to bless the visitors who had come to meet with them from a far country. My husband was asked to preach, and they asked me to sing. Because I never posed as a singer, I suggested that Alice and I sing a duet in Cinyanja. When we sang "When the Roll Is Called Up Yonder" in the Nyasaland vernacular, the people were so pleased that they asked us to repeat it.

We found them to be a wonderfully consecrated group of advent believers. When we sat that afternoon and talked over the beauties and wonders of our third angel's message, how their faces did shine! They would look from one to another almost speechless with the joy of their new-found faith. They shook their heads and said over and over again, "Why, it is wonderful, just wonderful!"

We shall never forget our long, eventful journey down from Nyasaland to South Africa. It was a wonderful beginning to the much-needed rest we are enjoying here at the seaside. Yes, we are resting, but our hearts still yearn over the black children we left behind us. They are precious, they are blood bought, and we trust our God to keep them as the apple of His eye.

God Speaks and the Earth Trembles

NIGHT was falling on a little heathen village up by the rippling waters of Lake Nyasa. Usually at this hour families were huddled about fires in their cookhouses, or in the *bwala* in the midst of the village. But tonight it was different. A strange pastor had come only that day to invite them to hear the "words of life." Every heathen heart was stirred with curiosity. Who was not interested in life? Had not that enemy, death, visited their village all too often, taking man and maid, the babes tied to the mothers' backs, as well as those old ones who were sickly and weak? Words of life! They would hear a saying or two about that.

The African evangelist had constructed a rough thatched prayer house, and thither the dark-skinned children of the bush pressed and seated themselves on the hard-packed earth.

The light from a flickering lantern shone fitfully on the faces of the audience upturned toward the young speaker. They were hearing strange things. The wrinkled Gogos and Bombos looked at one another in astonishment.

"Africa is in darkness, because we do not have the religion of Christ Jesus," the pastor had said earnestly. "All the greatest nations of the earth believe in the Lord Jesus

Christ. It is the heathen who have remained in darkness. Wherever the name of Jesus is taught, schools and churches come, and the children are taught a higher and better way to live."

There was much talk as the men and women made their way home that night.

"It is true that we do not know anything," they admitted. "And maybe this *mlendo* will tell us something we do not know."

Every night they pressed close together under the roof of the thatched house and listened, wonder growing in their hearts. At last the call came for these men and women to give up their sinful heathen practices and accept Jesus Christ.

That night Pastor Bexter had preached on the books of God. He had told them of the book of life and of the book of death.

"Every name is recorded somewhere," he said solemnly, "in the book of life or in the book of death!"

He wove into his sermon a graphic description of the New Jerusalem and the new earth. "None will ever enter there who love lies or superstition or heathenism," he declared. "No beer drinker will be there; no tobacco smoker."

Many pressed forward determined to give up all, that their names might be inscribed in the Lamb's book of life.

But one old woman hung back. When urged to give up all for the Lord Jesus, she only shook her woolly old head. Yes, yes, she believed, she told them. And she did want her name written in the book of life—but not yet—not *just* yet.

But when the young pastor, earnest and zealous, urged her, pleading wisdom and righteousness and judgment to come, she told him plainly why she was delaying.

"I have in my hut in the village many pots of *mowa* fermenting. Soon it will be ready for my friends to drink. I tasted it only today, and it is the best beer I have ever made. You say beer drinkers cannot have their names written in that book you are telling about. I will go home and have my beer dance. I will not waste this good beer I have made. But I will never make any more. Then I will come back when it is all gone and have my name put in that book of life."

Pleadings were in vain. She only shook her head and went silently back to her village through the blackness of the tropical night.

The next day she worked among the earthen pots, stirring her fermenting beverage of hell. That night her friends were to come and help her drink her last brewing of beer.

The next day she worked among the earthen pots, stirring her fermenting beverage of hell.

What thoughts scurried around in her old head as she hastened preparations for the night of orgy? No one will ever know, for at dusk, even as she was stirring, stirring—her old lips muttering gusty approval—there was a quick yellow flash from the bush, a hideous wailing scream, the crunching of bones, then silence. Her friends did not dare go to her rescue.

A few gnawed bones and some shredded remains of her dirty *nsaru* were all that were found of the old woman who was so foolish as to exchange her hope of eternal life for a drink of native beer.

Bewildered and filled with fear, she will arise in the second resurrection. She will see the City of God towering tier upon tier above her; she will wince when the glorious light from within wreathes the whole city with rainbows.

Her old body, bent with infirmities of labor and pain and age, once the food of wild beasts, will soon be food for flame—at her own choice. For she traded it all off—this ineffable glory of eternal life—for a drink of beer, a drink which was snatched from her lips before she had a chance to taste it.

"Whereas I Was Blind"

NOT LONG after Malamulo Mission was established in South Africa's Nyasaland, a little village school was started about ten miles east of the mission estate. It was known as Macheza school. It was a miserable place, looked at with satiated modern eyes—mud walls, mud floor, and grass roof. But it was here that little Captain Muluda Kanga learned to read and write.

He was a tiny lad with sparkling eyes and a quick active mind. He learned more here than just the three R's. He learned of the coming of the Lord. How his boyish heart thrilled when his native teacher told of the glorious day when even Africans who accept Christ would be taken to heaven as sons of God. He learned to keep the true Sabbath. He learned of the wonderful atonement of Jesus for the sins of the world.

Every Friday the young lad trudged home. And early Sabbath morning, when the family gathered about the big porridge pot for breakfast, Captain used to stand up and preach to them.

They gazed at this little one in deep pride and amazement. The small boy was already achieving great learning. Ah, well, these schools *were* wonderful. Then Captain took his brothers and went out into the villages to preach. Every Sabbath this small boy labored long and hard. He was determined then and there to be an evangelist, and he was alert in being about his heavenly Father's business.

One night he had a wonderful dream. He dreamed he was standing under the branches of a beautiful tree. Suddenly he heard a voice, sweet and melodious, saying, "Captain! Captain, come up! Come up!"

Filled with great eagerness, the lad began climbing the tree. When he got to the topmost branches, the voice was still insistent.

"Come up, Captain, come up."

He stood, clinging to the branches, listening.

"Captain," the voice continued, "do you know that there will be a great company of people who will be taken to heaven without tasting death? If you are faithful, Captain, you will be one of that number."

He awoke, thrilled with the ecstasy of his dream. The sweet musical voice sounded in his ears all the day long like a lovely refrain.

Soon after this he went to Malamulo Mission, which was then in its infancy. The few students could easily meet in the church. They had a mud-wall school at first, but it collapsed in a heavy rain, so the classes were moved into the church.

Just across the way was the hospital building. It was a small place, but the sick who came for help made a beaten trail to the door. Operations were performed while native boys held a sheet above the patient to keep dust, dirt, and bird droppings from falling from the grass roof into the wound. Here in this tiny building hundreds of Africans found healing and rest.

Captain was the laundry boy for the *gomi*. Early Friday

morning, with a bar of soap as long as his arm and a huge bundle of clothes on his head, he went down to the brook to do his work. Some of the boys had clothes made of bark in those days. The material was called *mkhwende,* and could be made clean and fresh by being soused in water repeatedly and then beaten on a smooth stone.

The laundry finished, he carried the clothes back and laid them on the clean grass to dry. Captain saw to it that every boy had clean things to wear on the Sabbath. There was no way to iron them, but they were clean, and altogether fitting by native standards.

The years fled by as if on wings, and Captain, with his wife and family, was in the midst of his chosen work. From village to village he trudged happily, telling the old, old story; bringing hope to a hopeless, downtrodden people. He preached the gospel, ministered to the sick, and helped to bury the dead.

People grew to look for the slim, earnest man who could tell them of a better way of life. Beer pots were hastily covered, and the twists of *fodia* were hidden when he came into a village. Tobacco and beer were out of place when Captain was there.

Suddenly it came over the good man that something was wrong with his eyes. He could hardly see to read his Bible any more, and each day it seemed as if the world grew dimmer. He labored with God in prayer over this thing, but darkness slowly closed in on the humble African preacher who had long since allowed the Sun of Righteousness to rule in his life.

He was sick with worry, yet he kept on his circuit faithfully, still holding on to the promises of God. Surely the heavenly Father whom he had trusted and for whom he had broken the bonds of heathenism would help him. Surely the loving Ruler of the universe would look down in pity upon His despairing child!

One terrible night Pastor Captain became lost in the bush. He had been detained late at a village where a poor mother lay desperately ill. The shadows of night were already slanting across the sky when he headed homeward. His bare feet felt desperately for the path his poor eyes could not see, though the sun had not yet sunk to rest. His heart sank within him. Could he ever find the way to his village? He was hungry and tired. He knew that Elie, his wife, would have a pot of *ndiwo* bubbling hot and waiting to pour on the thick, good *nsima* porridge that he loved. His mouth watered at the prospect of food, and his heart yearned for the love and the security he would find in his grass bush hut.

But suddenly he became aware that his feet had lost the path. He tried to find it, and became panicky, ran into a scraggly tree, and raked his shins on a fallen branch. After he had wandered in desperation for an hour or more, he stopped.

For whom were all those promises put into the Bible, if not for him?

"When thou passest through the waters, I will be with thee."

"Thou shalt tread upon the lion and the adder. . . ."

"Yea, though I walk through the valley of the shadow of death. . . ."

Captain was walking through the valley of the shadow even then, for in the black bush that surrounded him, leopards and lions, bloodthirsty and hungry, were hunting for prey.

The black minister knelt trembling in the rough grass, for all too well he knew how swift death can overtake a

As he knelt to pray, the roar of a
great lion fairly shook the ground.

hapless traveler lost in the bush. Only God could save him! But even as he knelt to pray, the roar of a great lion fairly shook the ground. The gentle breeze had wafted the "man smell" straight to the nostrils of the beast. Captain could hear the crackling of the underbrush as the huge creature crashed about, maddened with thirst for blood.

But there on his knees he claimed the promises of God. Then in perfect calm he lay down to sleep. All night the wild creatures of the African bush circled about him, searching, searching. They came so near that Captain felt as if he could reach out and almost touch their rough fur. But his trust in Jesus was complete, and God gave His beloved sleep. He kept him safely and helped him to find his way home in the morning.

This experience was repeated many times, until the light was gone from his eyes entirely. Then he was put on sustentation.

One night he had another dream. He saw Jesus, majestic and beautiful, sitting on the purple summit of Mount Mlanje. His glory was dazzling to behold. Then again he heard the sweet voice of the Saviour.

"Captain."

"Yes, Lord."

"Do you hear Me?"

"Yes, Lord."

"Do not worry about your eyes. I will take care of them. You take care about your soul."

This was repeated three times.

When he awoke, he got up weeping, and went outside the hut. He was not weeping for sorrow, but for joy. The burden was rolled away. He was at rest.

Last July Captain was called to be the chaplain of the Malamulo Mission Hospital. Now he knows why the Lord allowed him to go blind. No man with eyes could go about as freely through any hour of the day or night as Captain does.

During daylight hours his cane taps as he makes his round through the men's ward, the women's ward, and into the maternity hospital. He plods his kindly way through the "sick village," where those weary travelers stay who are taking treatments. He preaches every day in every ward. He prays at every bedside. Even in the Asiatic hospital, where Mohammedans hate the name of Jesus, he is welcome.

No one in all Africa can say that blessed name Jesus with more love and throbbing gratitude than old Captain. He kneels by the beds of Moslems, heathen, and Christians, and pleads for the presence and the blessing of the great Life-giver in behalf of the occupant. There are now twenty-nine persons in his hearers' class.

Old Captain may be blind, yes, but he is opening the eyes of the blind. He may have to be led by the hand over the maze of paths that lead hither and thither at Malamulo, but his hand is unwavering when he leads trembling fearful ones to the cross of Jesus Christ.

Little Glimpses of Mission Life

THE SUN beat down mercilessly on the rough mission road as my class and I started to climb the hill to the bean fields. They were that day to have a lesson on contour ridging and dike making, so that the rich soil on the hillsides would not wash into the valleys with every tropical downpour. We had seen too many rock-ribbed, barren hillsides already, and we were trying to educate the native people to prevent erosion in their own villages and mealie fields.

We were all chattering happily as we climbed, when suddenly we saw a bent little heathen woman coming down the road toward us. She was very old, and dragged one horny, calloused foot as she crept painfully along. Her gaunt body was wrapped in a ragged black *nsaru,* and tawdry brass bracelets jangled on her scrawny arms. Her face was as wrinkled as a prune, and there was a ring in her nose. I knew that that old black back had been twisted with pain, disease, and with the bearing of heavy loads of wood, water, and mealies for perhaps fourscore years.

On her woolly head just now was a great basket of *madea,* or the little rough husks left after pounding the soaked grains of corn. I rightly suspected that she was bound for the cattle *khola,* nearly a mile farther on, where she would be given a few precious handfuls of coarse salt for each basketful of *madea,* which makes excellent cattle feed.

The old grandmother was nearly exhausted, for the day was hot, and the load was very heavy. Already she had come three long miles across the bush, and the sweat dripped from her leathery black face. Her eyes had the drawn, desperate look of one who has come to the very tag end of her strength.

The old grandmother was nearly exhausted, for the day was hot, and the load was very heavy.

I stopped and spoke kindly to her. Old mothers ought to have a cool place to rest in the shade on such a hot day. Surely of all the babes that must have been bound to that bent back, one had grown up who would be glad and willing to bear her burdens and make her life easier in her old days! I thought of my precious mother back home in America, and great pity surged into my heart. Then I turned to my waiting students.

"Which one of you," I asked, "has enough love and pity in his heart to carry this *madea* to the *khola* for the old grandmother?"

Instantly one fine young man stepped forward.

"I will, madam," he said, and he took the heavy basket of husks from the head of the old heathen grandmother, put it on his own, and went marching off toward the *khola* with it.

African natives have a peculiar little thank-you gesture. They clap their hands softly while they duck their heads and murmur thank you again and again.

When the old woman crept up to me and began ducking her head and softly clapping her hands, I had the same feeling I once had when I went out into the road to pick up a poor injured dog. His eyes had looked into mine while he whined and licked my hands.

Then she hobbled after Nyasula, my student, who was making his way down the rocks toward the *khola*. In about thirty minutes he was with us again, his eyes gleaming like twin stars.

"Oh, I had a wonderful experience, madam; I must tell you," he cried, his black face shining as with an inward glory.

"While we were walking down to the *khola*, the old woman, who is named Gogo, spoke about how strong I am and how easily I was carrying her load.

" 'My boy,' she said, 'we have before us life and death. For you—life. For me—death. I have lived long; now there is only the grave before me, and nothing else. With me, all things will soon be over.' "

Then Nyasula burst out eagerly, "Ah, then, madam, I preached her a sermon on the coming of the Lord and the new earth. I told her, 'No, Gogo, the grave need not be the end of you. You can live forever if you want to. Even though you die here, and your body is buried in the ground, if you put away your sins, God will mark your grave and you will be raised to live forever. Then you, with all the precious children of God, may have a life without end!' "

The old woman had exclaimed in great wonder at the beautiful picture that Nyasula had drawn of the earth made new.

" 'Ah, my child,' she told me, 'these are strange words you are telling me. Do you mean that I, an old woman, no good to even my tribe or family any more, will rise out of the grave, and be young again? These are strange words, and hard for an old woman to believe!'

"I told her more about Jesus and how He died and made all these things possible for poor human beings, and how He went about healing the sick and comforting the poor when He was on earth.

" 'These missionaries,' she said, 'they must be *good* people. Some in our village say that the white man has come to Africa only to trouble us and to rob us; but I will see, my boy. I will think of this, and maybe I, too, can be raised up in the last day.' "

The old grandmother received her few handfuls of salt from the *khola,* but she received more than that. She had found a hope and a promise of something that is much better than salt, something which savoreth of eternal life.

*   *   *   *   *

I had a letter from big, black, happy Lincoln Chipunga a few days ago, and he told a story in it strangely similar to another story I heard a year or so ago. But knowing that the same old devil, the wily deceiver of the lowly and the lofty children of earth, is still busy, one need not be too surprised if history repeats itself occasionally.

Lincoln, a school inspector, walks many miles to bring hope, help, and courage to the heroic teachers of the pitiful little bush schools scattered all over his district. And Lincoln knows, as all our teachers know, that they are evangelists too. We depend upon them, not only to keep our schools in good running order and to disseminate knowledge to the children, but to preach the gospel of Jesus wherever and whenever they can.

Our black teachers sometimes are interrupted and annoyed. Often a meeting attracts not only those who wish to hear but also those who are there for mischief and disturbance.

One dark night while Lincoln was preaching, it seemed as if the very spirits of incensed devils were visible and moving about in the darkness. On the outskirts of the crowd, seated beneath a rude grass shelter, milled a rough restless element. *Mowa* flowed freely, and tongues were loosened in a babble of obscenity and profanity. A great fire had been kindled at one side to drive away mosquitoes and lighten the dense darkness. The firelight flickered on black, shining faces as the village folk listened to the message that Lincoln had brought to them. But he had to shout at the top of his voice to be heard above the bedlam. The meeting was drawing to a close, and in spite of the disturbances, hearts were being touched by his appeal.

"Give your hearts to Jesus Christ today," he pleaded. "Do not delay. Tomorrow may be too late. Every day, here in our country, people are dying in ignorance. Decide now, my brothers, to give up all for the Lord Jesus Christ."

Just then a harsh burst of laughter rang out, and a great black, half-naked man elbowed his way in under the grass shelter.

"I have been listening to you, Teacher," he said in a loud

voice, "and I believe you are right. I have been a wicked man, but I would like to have this Jesus that you speak of. He sounds good to my heart. I will come back in a day or two and talk to you about Him."

Lincoln looked into the restless eyes of the huge native and realized that the Spirit of God was struggling here for supremacy. Even then the hands of his companions were reaching out to draw him back to them. The jeering became thunderous.

Lincoln was at his side immediately and grasped his hard, black hand. *"Mbale okondedwa"* (beloved brother)—I can almost hear him speak—"decide today. Forsake the *mowa*. Leave your evil companions. We cannot tell. Tomorrow may be too late."

But the man looked nervously back at his laughing confederates, and wavered. His pride would not allow a complete surrender now.

"I'll come back, Teacher. Truly I will. Nothing will happen to me. See? I am very strong. I worked six years in the gold mines at Johannesburg and four years at Kimberley. Men died at work such as I have done, but I only became stronger." He beat on his great chest and flexed his rippling muscles to show Lincoln that he was sure of the morrow. He was too strong to die, so he thought.

"I will come back alone tomorrow. You wait for me. I must learn more of this Jesus. I feel it here," he said, pressing a great fist against his heart. "I never felt so before. I must have this happiness—this great peace that you speak of. But not tonight."

Lincoln put a small tract into his hand, and he looked at it a moment in bewilderment. Then without a word he went off with his friends into the outer darkness that was spiritual as well as literal.

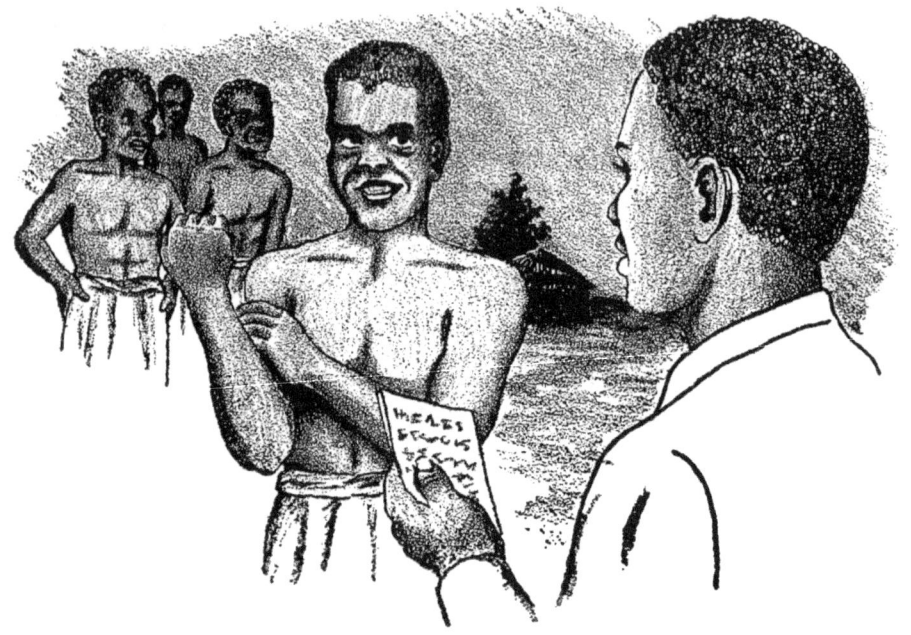

He beat on his great chest and flexed his rippling muscles to show Lincoln that he was sure of the morrow.

Lincoln turned back to his waiting congregation. Things were quiet and peaceful now, and his voice could easily be heard. But the teacher seemed deeply moved. A strange premonition told him that though the young man had promised most earnestly to return, yet he would never look upon his face again.

As the people went quietly back to their mud huts in the village, the throb of drums in a nearby village advertised that a beer dance was in progress. All night the diabolical drums throbbed, and Lincoln moved uneasily in his sleep. Even in his dreams came the thoughts of soul winning and the heartbreak it often entails.

All through the next day Lincoln waited for the man to return, but he did not come. At length the sun sank over the western rim of the world, and again the curtain of the tropical night dropped over the land. Lincoln rolled out his mat and lay down to sleep.

The next morning a group of half-sober men from the adjoining village staggered up the bush path. Their eyes were wide with fear. There had been strangers in their village for a day and a night, drinking beer with them, they said.

This morning a little boy had discovered one of them in the bush. Evidently he had lain down to sleep, and a lion had found him. "He had this in his hand when the boy saw him, and when we heard that there was a preacher in this village, we brought it to you. Maybe you will know who this stranger was."

They held out to Lincoln the tattered remains of a little tract—the paper he had placed in the hand of the young man who was so sure of the morrow. The messengers wavered off uncertainly, and Lincoln stood looking after them with unshed tears in his eyes. He knew that again the wretched beer pots had barred a soul from the gates of gold and from the way of the tree of life.

*   *   *   *   *

The evangelistic and teachers' institute we had been holding at Luwazi Mission was almost over. We had been "camping" in the empty mission house so reminiscent of the beloved presence of Pastor and Mrs. W. L. Davy. For three weeks Pastors Webster Pierce and L. A. Edwards and I had been working on institute topics while Mrs. Webster "held the fort" and kept us supplied with most delicious food.

Mothers, fathers, sisters, brothers, grandmothers, aunts, and uncles of my students, past and present, at Malamulo. kept the path up the hill warm, paying us their respects. Their regards usually took a concrete form, for they brought us eggs, sweet potatoes, tangerines, pumpkins, and peanuts. One old Ngoni mother, thin as a rake, came up the hill with a dish of eggs on her head. After we had accepted them with thanks, and indulged in the peculiar handshake of this region, she leaned toward me, her thin face quivering with earnestness.

"*Ali bwanji Penazi?*" (How is Penazi?) she asked.

Ah, the age-old mother love! I looked into her eyes, made bleary by the smoke of ten thousand kitchen fires, and assured her that her Penazi was well and was a good boy. Her wrinkled face splintered into smiles, and she went away, only to return soon again with a gift of peanuts and sweet potatoes for the teacher of her beloved Penazi.

During our last week at Luwazi, Robertson, our Mala-mulo-trained medical assistant, came up to the mission house.

"There has come a most terrible case to our dispensary," he said. "As for me, I can do nothing. Oh, that we had a doctor at Luwazi! But there is no doctor anywhere in this part of the country, madam. But come down and see this poor old grandmother. It is terrible—awful—yet I must turn her away."

Mrs. Webster and I walked down the hill to the little burned-brick dispensary. A motley group of sufferers waited with the age-old patience of their race for the *mankhwala* to cure their malaria and dysentery and a hundred other diseases which torment their lives.

The old grandmother stood a little apart from the rest and nervously shifted her ragged *nsaru* a little tighter about her lean loins. Her stomach was swollen almost to the bursting point, and her legs were running with dropsical sores. The flies and gnats enveloped her in a buzzing black cloud. In her eyes we saw only hopelessness.

"I can wash her wounds and send her back to die," said Robertson sadly. "I can do no more."

Evangelism in the Wilderness

NEAR the slopes of beautiful Cholo Mountain, with its dozens of small native villages, we decided to have an effort. Not a tent effort, no, but an effort just the same, for where could we find any *hema* or tents in Central Africa?

Near to one of our small bush schools, the people built us a house. Oh, it was a fine house, made entirely of grass. It was not for protection from the rain (for it never rained at this season of the year), but rather for protection from prying eyes, from prowling beasts, and a slight protection from the sun—but not much.

Then, we had a list at the mission house of things we must take when we went out on those efforts. Soap (hand and laundry), matches, kerosene, meal, flour, oil, shortening, mosquito nets, towels (hand, tea), quinine, atabrine, powdered milk, egg beater, etc., etc. It was necessary to have a good supply of such things.

We took our few essentials to our grass hut in the mission "lorry"—our camp cots, a folding table, foot tub for baths, wash basins, and a little primus stove on which to cook our food if it was too windy to cook it over a fire. One of my treasured possessions was a folding skillet of cast aluminum.

In this, Andy made biscuits, even corn bread, right on coals over an open fire.

My dearest treasure was my folding organ—a present from a man in Minneapolis. He will have stars in his crown because of that present, for the beauty of the music kept our audience large every night of the whole six weeks.

I'd just set it up under the sky, in the open, hard-beaten courtyard, and begin to play as meeting time approached. We didn't need to beat on drums or ring bells! The people heard the sweet, reedlike tones of my pretty organ, and how they ran to be near and to see as well as hear! In their starved lives, the music of their drums and of their voices was all they had ever heard.

One old fellow, with only a ragged blanket wrapped

One old fellow, with only a ragged blanket wrapped around him, crept near to me.

around him, crept near to me. His old black face was wreathed in smiles.

"*Nyimbo za kumwamba,*" he whispered.

"No, old father," I answered. "This is not the music of heaven. Oh, no! 'Eye hath not seen, nor ear heard, . . . the things which God hath prepared for them that love him.' "

Every day my husband with his native evangelists went out from village to village to preach to the people. Andy stayed at our camp to carry water from a water hole half a mile away, and to boil it and strain it for us to drink. I usually took a bath in the grass roofless bath house. My utensils were a dipper and a pot of water, a wash cloth and a cake of soap.

It was *so* hot. Five minutes after I had bathed, I needed another bath. I felt sorry for the evangelists and my husband tramping the miles and miles between villages in the boiling sun.

One morning a native teacher came to see me. I said to him, "Oh, I wish I had some oranges! They would taste *so* good!"

That night I had about one-half bushel of oranges. This faithful teacher had gone almost twenty miles to get them. We were constantly made aware of devotion such as this.

On the last day of the effort, it thundered all day. I said, "Oh, if it rains, we'll be drenched! This hut roof won't turn water! You can see the sky through it."

But everyone said, "But it doesn't ever rain in October. The rains come in November. Do not worry. It won't rain!"

But after the meeting that night it was so threatening and the thunder and lightning was so constant that we decided to load everything that rain would spoil into our jeep station wagon and go home, across the valley to Malamulo about nineteen miles away. We would not wait until morning.

It was a lucky thing that we did. Before we had gotten out of the bad mountain roads onto the better, more-traveled Cholo road, the rain was coming down by the bucketful, in gusts and freshets. Our organ, books, bedding and clothes were all dry. So were Andy and I and my husband. We all congratulated one another that we decided to do this.

We had won one hundred and one precious souls to the kingdom of God; we had spent six weeks right out in the heart of the bush where we could hear the wild animals crying at night. And notably, we saw it really rain in October!

While we were gone, our substitute cook boy, Cameron Msumba, had cleaned the kitchen, scoured the woodwork, canned two hundred quarts of mulberries, twenty-five quarts of peaches, thirty quarts of tomatoes, some guavas, and made some jelly.

Laiton Chirombo, the houseboy, had put clean sheets on our beds, and all of our clothes were clean and pressed. The whole house was airy, cool, and clean.

We heard the native gossip we had missed during our brief exile. A lion had appeared one night at the evangelist's village, scaring the native women into fits. A leopard came to the hen house every night but couldn't get in, of course. Betsey wanted to set. The turkey hen had laid six eggs in an old straw basket out in the bush. The tom-turkey insisted on sleeping on the roof of the hen house every night, but had to be evicted with clods of earth and pieces of turf. The old fellow would be a toothsome morsel for the visiting leopard.

Well, well, well! It was good to be home. Very good indeed.

Home looked pretty good after those six weeks of primitive life. The big white porcelain kerosene refrigerator looked very good indeed. The cold, firm butter, the ice cubes, the crisp lettuce, the cool tomatoes, gave us fresh heart and courage. We thought of the early missionaries who had none of the simple creature comforts we were thankful for. It gave us more respect for those who had paved the way, for they had had to live *all the time* as we had lived for the past six weeks.

Dailo

L ONG ago, some of the schools in Africa were not very good. Sometimes, a man who could hardly read himself would think he knew enough to teach children to read and write. He thought he might earn a little money in this way and set himself up as a great man. One such man set himself up as a teacher in a village. The people did not know that he was a cheat, because they did not know how to read or write or count or figure themselves.

Dailo was sent to school by his widowed mother. She wanted her small boy to learn much and be a clever man when he grew up. But day after day went by, and Dailo did not learn anything. After the teacher had given them some physical exercise, he taught them gardening. In this, they all hoed in the teacher's garden. Then the teacher taught them singing, going over songs they all knew already. Then he taught them games. They all went through jumping and dancing games they all knew better than the teacher knew them. Then a short time before they went home, the teacher hung up a ragged old chart, and had the children say words after him, as *"ona, ana, Onani, ana, Onanso, Mwana."*

Dailo had no idea in the world what it all was about, and neither did the other children for that matter. No one was learning anything, but the teacher's garden was very big and was growing fine.

When the parents complained, the teacher got very mysterious and told them that learning to read and to write was very, very hard, and would take a long time.

One day a cousin of Dailo came to visit them. It was a girl. She was attending a mission school on the other side of the mountain. Akufani was her name. She brought her small reader along—the one she used at the mission school. She told Dailo and his mother that the name of it was "Moyo wa Kristu," or the "Life of Christ."

"Can you read any words yet?" asked Dailo's mother curiously.

"Can you read any words yet?"
asked Dailo's mother curiously.

"Oh, yes!" cried Akufani, and she eagerly seized her little book and began to read aloud without any hesitation at all.

"Yohane wababza anakhale kale mu dzeko la pansi. Anakhala mu dzeko bna. Anakhala kwawa pamene—"

"Stop," cried the mother. "How many years have you been learning that you are able to read like you are even talking?"

"I started just this year."

"This year!" screamed the mother. "Then I will take a bamboo and beat this pig I have for a son. He is a great waster of time and substance. I paid that teacher a goat, some sweet potatoes, and two fat hens. And look at him! He can do nothing!"

Dailo was so scared he was ready to run for the bush to escape a beating. Yet he was very puzzled. How could a person learn? He had listened with all his heart. How could it be done?

But Akufani spoke up then, to save the boy.

"Listen to my words, Mother, and do not beat the boy, for I have heard of this teacher, that he is a cheat, and cannot read so very well himself. I wonder if he could even read this small book I am reading, yet it is for the first class."

"Then what will he do in another year," inquired the mother, "when we are all angry that our children do not learn?"

"Oh, he will say he is sick, or something like that. You will see. But I'll tell you what to do!"

"What? What?" asked Dailo, for he truly wanted to learn.

"You come go with me. I'll speak for you at the mission station, and they will take you. Then you'll see how quick you can learn to read. And write, too, for that matter."

The next morning, early, Dailo, and his cousin Akufani

started over the mountain to the mission station where the boy laid all his hopes of learning to read. Even though he was five months late, with Akufani's help, he soon caught up, and pretty soon, he was the brightest one in the whole class.

After he had recited one day, the teacher said to him, "You, Dailo, I think when you grow up, you will be a teacher!"

Looking up at the kind schoolmaster, Dailo decided then and there that that was what he wanted to be.

When he went home that year's end, he took two books, *Moyo wa Kristu* and *Tupi la Kristu,* and he read them both to his mother. Because one was on the life of Jesus Christ, and the other on his death for our sins, she was converted by hearing the words her son read, and later, when Dailo was baptized, his mother was baptized, too.

Love Makes the Way

I TRIED all the time I was in Africa to convert my cookboy, Andy Sandula. But he would not accept Christianity. He would go to baptismal class for a few weeks, but then he'd get tired, and quit. It did not seem so very important to him. But we all know that accepting Christ is a life and death matter.

Andy was a splendid cook. He could make beautiful pies, cakes, and bread. He knew how to set the table, and iron the clothes until they were as smooth as glass. He made lovely salads and folded napkins in all kinds of fancy shapes. He loved to make them look like white rabbits in my drinking glasses.

But he was a queer one, too. If I had a guest or a family visiting me whom he did not like, he was sure to burn something or be very, very late with the food.

Finally, one day, after my dinner was a total failure, I went into the kitchen and looked at him hard and long. He would not meet my eye.

"Why do you do this," I asked, "every time certain people come?"

He would not meet my eye. Finally he said, "They do not like Africans."

One day, after my dinner was a total failure, I went
into the kitchen and looked at him hard and long.

"Well," I said, "I heard them talking. They said they felt
very sorry for me."

"Why?" asked Andy in astonishment.

"They said I have such a bad cook, it is a big wonder I
do not get sick and die."

"But I do not cook this way every day," he protested. "I
do not like to cook good things for them."

"But then you spoil your good name," I said. "They are
telling everyone what a bad cook you are. And when I go
back to America, you might not get a good job."

He looked at me a long time. Then his face broke into
smiles.

"I see!" he said, "I see. Well I will always try to cook
good food for everybody."

"That's fine," I said, "and I'm glad. You know, the Bible

247

says, 'Love your enemies. Do good unto them that despitefully use you and persecute you.' "

But whenever I spoke about Christianity to Andy, he looked uneasy, and acted as if he didn't want to talk about it. He tried to change the subject.

One day when I was talking, he told me, "When I first saw a motor car, I thought it was a new kind of terrible wild beast, and I ran off into the bush and did not go home all day."

Then he said that when the white people first came into that section of Africa, people all said they were a kind of fish, because they came out of the sea. He said he thought at first that the skin of the white people was so tender they would bleed if they were touched.

The day we left Malamulo to return to America was a sad one indeed. All of those who worked for us were there, and were weeping. We were weeping too. Then I said to Andy, "Oh, Andy, I don't think I'll see you in the kingdom of heaven, for you are not a Christian. I'll see Waison, and Lester, and Cirombo, and Whiteson—but you, Andy—you won't be saved unless you accept Jesus as your Saviour!"

Then Andy began to cry.

"You have been so good to me, Madam, I want to see you again!"

"And I want to see you too, Andy. Oh, why won't you give your heart to Jesus?"

"Kapena! Kapena [perhaps, perhaps]!" he sobbed.

I had been in America some months when I had an impression that I should send a box to Andy—a box of clothes for him and his family.

I packed it and mailed it. I knew it would take nearly two months for it to get to Central Africa.

I had a suit of clothes for Andy, with some shirts, neckties, and some handkerchiefs. There were dresses for his plump little wife, and dresses for his two daughters. I put in a pound of soft brown sugar as a treat. Then I waited. I knew Andy would write and thank me as soon as he got it, for he has better manners than many of the Christians.

Sure enough, in about three months, here came my letter. He had written as soon as he received the parcel, just as I knew he would.

"Dear Madam, [he wrote]

"I was very happy to receive the parcel from you with presents for my whole family. We were very much surprised to know that you still are remembering us, even though you have returned to your own country.

"When I got that, and realized you spoiled [spent] much money for me, I thought, 'This is love. This is love like the love of Christ she has told me of.' You'll be glad to know our whole family are to be baptized. This is because of love.

"Your boy,
"Andy"

And love is the secret. Love is the way. There is no other way to win souls.

Chirombo Family

I HAD three of the Chirombo boys to work for me. The first was Waison, a bashful, silent boy who did his work faithfully and well. Even though he was a good Christian, Waison could hardly get over some of his superstitious fears. One day, I found a big chameleon in my yard. He was about eighteen inches long. I got him and took him into the house to look at him and enjoy him.

But, oh dear! I went in one door with the chameleon, and Waison burst out the other one, his eyes bulging with fear.

"Nthumanzi! Nthumanzi [dreadful! dreadful!]!" he cried.

I asked him why, but I couldn't get any sensible talk out of him, so I just had to put the chameleon outdoors if I expected to get any work done that day. But I asked and asked, and finally I found out why he was so afraid of the chameleon. Pastor James Ngaiyaye, an old veteran in God's work, told me.

He said that Africans have an old legend relating to the very beginning of the world. Long ago, when man first committed sin, death came upon the earth. Man was very frightened by this strange thing called "death." It was *nthumanzi*. But the great God up in heaven felt pity for man, and He wanted to send him a message of hope. So He called the chameleon.

"Chameleon," said the great God, "men on the earth are filled with great fear because of this thing called death. Now, since you can travel very fast, I want you to take a message to man. Tell him that even though he dies, he can live again. Death is not an eternal sleep. I will wake them up into a brighter, better, happier life, where there is no sin. Go tell that to man for Me."

But the chameleon was a creature which was slow to obey. He had no pity for men who were sighing and crying about the terrible thing called death. So he went very slowly and reluctantly on the errand of the Lord.

But Mdierekezi, the devil, heard the gentle words of God the loving Father.

"Do you hear that?" he cried in great anger. "Now God wants to comfort man and give him hope after I have made him to sin and plunged him into despair."

"Come here, you!" cried Mdierekezi to the lizard. "I have an errand for you. And I want you to go very fast and beat chameleon to the earth. Now listen!

"You go to the earth and tell the people that death is eternal and everlasting! Tell them the grave is the end of everything. Tell them all men must die and there is no hope of another life! Tell them! Tell them! Go! Quick!" he shouted in a voice like thunder.

The lizard scuttled away to the earth with this terrible message. And when the people heard it, they cried louder than ever and found no comfort in anything. After a long while, here came chameleon. They listened to his weak little story.

"You are too late!" the people cried. "Your story cannot be true, for you have come so late."

And that is the reason the people hate chameleon—he came too late to bring joy and hope to the people. No wonder poor little superstitious Waison hated chameleons!

One day Leckion, my houseboy, brought a witch doctor's clothes and mask for me to see. It was a horrible mask, carved out of wood, with whiskers made of the hair of goats. There was a grass skirt he wore, too. Leckion put these things on and began to jump around to show me just how the witch doctors do their dances. Just then Waison came in. When he saw the terrible-looking creature prancing around in my kitchen, grass skirt flying, wooden mask grinning horribly, he screamed terribly, and started again to run.

"*Nthumanzi! Nthumanzi!*" he screamed, darting for the door.

When Waison saw the terrible-looking creature prancing around in my kitchen, he screamed terribly.

I seized him and held him. "Don't run," I said. "This is not a real *mfiti* [witch], but just Leckion Cosalawa dressed up like *mfiti!*"

He had reason to fear *mfiti,* for these wicked men will even kill for money—and often as not cook and eat their victims, if they can do so without being caught by the watchful government. They know poisons so quick and so potent that even wise scientists have been unable to find out what they are. Yes, Waison is not foolish to fear *mfiti.* It is a craft of the devil, and we need to fear him too with all our hearts.

Lester came to work for me later, when Waison was lent to a new missionary who needed him. Lester Chirombo was Waison's brother. He was very poor when he came, and his clothes were in rags and tatters.

One day a box of clothing came to me from America. There was clothing that just fitted Lester, and he was the happiest boy at Malamulo when he got these clothes on in place of the old rags he had worn. Then Lester brought his brother Laiton to be my houseboy, for Leckion, my first houseboy, had begged leave to go to a school to learn tailoring.

Laiton was a real character. He was grinning, laughing, happy, and gay most of the time. But one day, he had a terrible fall on his bicycle and had jagged wounds and bruises all over his legs and arms.

His elbows and knees looked like raw meat when he limped up to the house that morning. When I told him to go to the mission hospital so it could be dressed, his eyes filled with fear.

"Oh, no! Oh, no!" he cried.

I knew that the heathen tell that we kill the native people in the hospital and make them into medicine, so I didn't urge further. I tore long strips of bandaging and cleansed and dressed all those wounds myself. His gratitude knew no bounds.

Some weeks later, when Lester was stricken with the terrible tick fever, I put him into the hospital, though he protested loudly against going. In a day or so he was telling everyone that the hospital was a wonderful place—not like the people say at all.

While Lester was ill, Laiton did his and Lester's work too. One day when Andy was sick, he did the work of three. He tried to make a pie that day, but the crust was so tough it nearly broke our teeth to eat it. But I did not find fault. He did the best he could. And all of the servants were so excited about it. The garden boy said to me when I returned from school:

"Laiton *wapanga* pie!" (Laiton made a pie.)

The girl who sewed for me said:

"Laiton *wapanga* pie!"

The wood and water boy said:

"Laiton *wapanga* pie!"

There was a little window between the dining room and kitchen where the dishes were put through. I saw a beaming black face watching us closely as we attacked that pie— beaming and joyful that he could serve us. I was glad we did not hurt his feelings, and chewed down and swallowed that tough crust.

I always loved to change my furniture around to different positions in the house. It seems as if the room is cleaner if I have a general upset once in a while. Laiton was quick to sense this. My husband, to tease me, told a guest once that he slept on the sewing machine all night one night and it was morning before he realized that I had changed the bed to another corner of the room.

One day I came home from school and heard a big disturbance in the front room. Laiton had the naive habit of talking to himself and laughing inordinately while he worked. I heard him emitting huge guffaws of laughter and saying again and again, *"Adzacikonda! Adzacikonda!"* (She will like this! She will like this!)

Standing there, I made up my mind that I *would*—no matter what he did, where he put things, I *would* like it, for people are worth so much more than things. Things will wear out and perish and can be thrown away, but people can have eternal life.

When I slipped into the kitchen, I saw Andy just bent double with laughter.

"Just wait, Madam," he chuckled. "He is changing the sitting room and he thinks you will really like it."

"I will!" I answered firmly.

Poor Laiton! He hadn't had any training in either artistry or balance in arrangement. One end of the room was simply glutted with furniture, while the other end had practically nothing. The piano stood in front of one of the windows.

I liked it, because it was a product of love and devotion and an earnest, wholesome desire to please me. I thought about my own efforts to please the Lord and how bungling and unlearned and awkward they must be before His magnificent intelligence. And I prayed that I might become as a little child—as naive, wholesome, and artless as Laiton Chirombo.

I saw Waison, Lester, and Laiton all led down into the Nambichamba River, below the dam, and baptized. And because they are trying every day in their humble ways to serve the Lord, I believe they will each have a crown that will never fade away, some glad day.

TEACH Services, Inc.
P U B L I S H I N G

We invite you to view the complete
selection of titles we publish at:
www.TEACHServices.com

We encourage you to write us
with your thoughts about this,
or any other book we publish at:
info@TEACHServices.com

TEACH Services' titles may be purchased in
bulk quantities for educational, fund-raising,
business, or promotional use.
bulksales@TEACHServices.com

Finally, if you are interested in seeing
your own book in print, please contact us at:
publishing@TEACHServices.com
We are happy to review your manuscript at no charge.

www.ingramcontent.com/pod-product-compliance
Lightning Source LLC
Chambersburg PA
CBHW071831020726
47502CB00004B/1321

* 9 7 8 1 4 7 9 6 1 6 8 2 4 *